YOUR
HIGH-PERFORMANCE
GUIDE to STUDY
and LEARNING

Scott Francis
Michael C Nagel

 20 key habits for getting the most out of your study time

amba
press

Published in 2023 by Amba Press, Melbourne, Australia
www.ambapress.com.au

Previously published in 2020 by Hawker Brownlow Education.
This edition replaces all previous editions.

ISBN: 9781922607966 (pbk)
ISBN: 9781922607973 (ebk)

A catalogue record for this book is available from the National Library of Australia.

Dedication

To my wife Sam, who inspires me through who she is as a person and as a teacher, and with whom the journey, both metaphorically and through our travel, is the reward.

My fondest professional journey has been with the two cohorts where I was a year level coordinator – during Year 9 and 10 with the seniors of 2014 at Bowen State High School, and during Year 10, 11 and 12 with the seniors of 2018 at The Lakes College.

Many thanks,

Scott

To my wife, Laura. All that I am able to achieve occurs through the support of my partner in life! Every day is always better with you!

Michael

Acknowledgements

I would like to acknowledge Michael Nagel, who started my interest in many of the topics in this book when I was a student in his class at the University of the Sunshine Coast, and who both encouraged and co-wrote this book. I would also like to acknowledge and thank the professional colleagues that I have worked with at Bowen State High School, Beerwah State High School, The Lakes College and Balmoral State High School – I find teaching a tremendously collegial profession and I am grateful for the rich professional experiences that I have enjoyed with my colleagues during my teaching journey.

Scott Francis

I, in return, would like to thank Scott for his passion and for the opportunity to work with him on this worthwhile project. He is truly an inspirational educator!

Michael C Nagel

Finally we would both like to thank the team at Hawker Brownlow Education, Olivia, Mark and Jacinta, who supported and guided the production of the book in a thoughtful, professional and enthusiastic manner.

Table of contents

About the authors

Scott Francis is a high-school teacher currently teaching business, legal studies and mathematics in Brisbane. He has previously taught in North Queensland at Bowen State High School, on the Sunshine Coast at Beerwah State High School and in the Brisbane area at The Lakes College and Balmoral State High School. Scott has held various roles in schools including deputy head of secondary, year-level coordinator, head of department and classroom teacher. He studied teaching at the University of the Sunshine Coast, completing a Graduate Diploma of Education before completing a Master of Education at Queensland University of Technology.

Scott also has a background in personal finance, having written the book *High Income Investing*, published by Wilkinson Publishing, and monthly articles for the online publication *Eureka Report*.

Away from teaching Scott enjoys fishing, basketball and travelling.

Dr Michael C Nagel is an Associate Professor at the University of the Sunshine Coast where he researches and teaches in the areas of child and adolescent development, behaviour, and educational psychology. A prolific author, Dr Nagel has written fourteen books related to human development and education with particular interest in the developing pediatric brain, behaviour and learning.

Along with being a contributor to a number of textbooks used in undergraduate and postgraduate education courses throughout Australia and abroad, Dr Nagel has been nominated as Australian Lecturer of the Year each year since 2010 and has been an invited expert on *Breakfast, Sunrise, A Current Affair* and *The Project*. Dr Nagel is also a member of the prestigious International Neuropsychological Society and a feature writer for *JiGSAW* and *Child* magazines, which collectively offer parenting and educational advice to more than one million Australian readers.

When he is not busy professionally, he spends his time learning the important lessons of life from his amazing partner, Laura, and his own children, Madeline and Harrison.

Introduction

Earlier this year I read an interesting article – a teacher in the US won $10 000 just by reading the terms and conditions of her travel insurance. The travel insurance company was making the point that very few people actually read the terms and conditions of travel policies, and it took the rather extreme step of putting a $10 000 prize in the terms and conditions to see if someone would read that far. Perhaps more interesting was a report from the UK that a wi-fi company included a checkbox for customers to agree to 'assign their first born to us for the duration of eternity' when signing up and had six people click on it – although the company did acknowledge that it was 'probably not enforceable'. I fear that introductions to books might be a little like the poor unread terms and conditions – but can you afford not to read this introduction when it has started with a vague connection to a similar situation that had a significant prize hidden somewhere?

What is this book about?

This book contains twenty key methods to get the most out of your study and learning time. This is the core focus of the book – how to be more effective when you are spending time studying and learning.

The ideas in the book have many parallels with other high-performance environments such as sport or music – the importance of setting goals, practicing effectively, using sleep and exercise to enhance performance, thinking about your mindset and building routines to support performance (for example, exam routines). Each reader will get something different from this book. Certain readers may already be practicing some of the strategies presented in this book and may adopt just a few new habits to enhance their learning. Others may choose to overhaul their existing study and learning philosophies to create for themselves a high-performance environment.

It should be stressed that this book is about being effective when you study and learn, rather than spending hour after hour working away. There are so many other elements to life beyond study that are important – work, family, friends, sport, culture – that it makes sense that when you are choosing to sit down and study, you do it with intensity and efficiency.

Who are the authors?

I am a high-school teacher who has an interest in the study and learning skills that students can build to support successful learning. This started while I was an impatient student in my early twenties. I found a way to enrol myself in both an undergraduate and postgraduate degree at the same time and, instead of completing the usual four subjects as a full-time load for a semester, I completed eleven. It forced me to think about how we learn efficiently and sparked my interest in how we can get the most out of our learning endeavours. The confidence I built as a student allowed me to complete six university degrees, four of them master's degrees, while being awarded a number of academic awards.

Later, as a teacher the topic of learning and study skills became an area of interest, further research, and discussion and experimentation with the students that I taught. While I was studying to be a teacher, I took one of Michael Nagel's classes around the topic of learning and how the brain works, which further inspired my interest in the subject and led to his involvement with this book, providing an expert opinion in each chapter.

Nagel's area of expertise is neuroscience and education. In each chapter he provides a comment on the topic being discussed. By doing so he adds an expert's view about how the brain functions and what that means for us as we learn. Such a view from someone who is a highly regarded expert in the field is a tremendous addition to the book.

The structure of the book

The book has twenty chapters, organised into four sections:

- The first section looks at topics around mindset and challenges you to be deliberate about the way you choose your attitudes toward learning. This includes thinking about stress, your attitude to learning or mindset, the importance of doing the things you enjoy, the value of 'academic intensity' and how motivation can work for you.

- The second section is focused on planning and routines. This starts by looking at the evidence that suggests that setting and writing down goals is a great planning mechanism to improve results. The section then moves on to look at another key planning element, 'spacing' your revision efforts over time, before finally considering the routines and planning needed to be successful in tackling assignments and exams.

- The third section deals with high-impact study techniques, giving you some specific ideas about how you might tackle study tasks. These high-impact study techniques include using feedback, graphic organisers, practice questions and handwriting.

- The fourth section moves to the topic of brain-based learning strategies and challenges you to think about how the brain learns and how you might tailor your study to better suit this. This includes thinking about topics as diverse as attention spans, the importance of sleep, social learning, the positive impact of exercise and the negative impact that multitasking has on learning.

And lastly, I apologise for any implied misrepresentations about possible prizes that have kept you reading all the way though the introduction, but I appreciate your interest and hope you get something out of this book that helps make your journey as a student more efficient and successful.

SECTION 1
Choosing your mindset

CHAPTER 1

Thinking about your attitude to 'stress'

*The greatest weapon against stress is our ability
to choose one thought over another.*
William James, philosopher and psychologist

The power of thinking about your attitude to 'stress'

There is an important word that we need to know to challenge a lot of thinking about the concept of stress, and that is *eustress*. Eustress introduces us to the desirable aspects of stress and refers to the positive changes that are brought about from stepping out of our comfort zone and taking on challenges (public speaking, leadership, a course of study) that feel uncomfortable but lead to growth. Understanding that a healthy amount of stress can lead to positive outcomes can help us challenge some of the assumptions that stress and study will always be linked and have an overarching negative impact on us while we are learning.

How attitudes to stress can enhance learning

In 2019, the University of the Sunshine Coast lecturer Shelley Davidow was quoted as saying, 'I don't know why we glorify stress. We think that if we show we are stressed at school, university or work that we're working hard, that if you're up late at night it must mean you're doing a good job, it's totally incorrect' (Cassidy, 2019, 'Stress should not be glorified' section).

This is the element of stress that I want to challenge in your thinking – the way we tend to glorify and misunderstand stress as part of the learning process. As Davidow alludes to, we don't need to 'lean into' this celebration of stress. We need to be aware of how damaging the impacts of negative stress, distress, can be to learning.

Nagel and Scholes (2016) provide a comparison of eustress and distress: 'Optimum levels of stress, referred to as eustress, can act as powerful empathetic, motivational and creative forces while negative, chronic or traumatic stress (distress) is potentially very destructive for the body and mind' (p. 297).

Clearly, we want to avoid distress. A high level of stress leads to a phenomenon referred to as *downshifting*, where the fight-or-flight reaction of the brain reduces the capacity of the brain to think due to high levels of stress hormones. This can happen in learning-related environments, including exams and study, or can happen in other environments that then affect your learning (as an example, think about trying to concentrate in a class after having an argument with a friend). If you are in a position where you feel the level of stress you are exposed to is impairing your abilities as a student, for example, your ability to perform at a reasonable level in exams or your ability to study and retain information, you should seek help, whether it be from your doctor, counselling services or by discussing it with trusted adults.

This chapter deals more with what I have observed at both high school and university: the tendency of student culture to focus on the concept of stress and see it as an entirely negative phenomenon; the tendency to hear the phrase 'I'm so stressed' bouncing around from conversation to conversation between students; the tendency of students to see stress as inevitable and to glorify the role of stress as part of being a 'good' student.

I want to build on the idea that a level of stress might be a good thing. If I wanted to eliminate all stress, I could sit on the couch all day, watch television and reflect on just how comfortable pyjamas really are – it would be a low-stress life, and a low-achievement one as well. This is where the idea of eustress becomes useful – having a concept that allows us to understand that a level of challenge, a level of stress, is indeed positive.

Kelly McGonigal is a Stanford University health psychologist who considers the way our attitude to stress, our mindset, can help turn a stressful event into a positive outcome. In a 2013 presentation, McGonigal discussed a study of people who were put through mock job interviews that were intentionally made to be stressful. The interviewees were split into two groups. One group watched a video before their interview that talked about how stress can be positive – including by improving performance, enhancing wellbeing and helping you grow. Those people who watched the video and received the positive information about stress had a greater release of DHEA (dehydroepiandrosterone, a neurosteroid that helps the brain grow stronger from challenges) during their interviews than the group who had not seen the video. The video helped that group have a positive experience out of the stressful situation. McGonigal also cites other research that suggests that viewing a stressful situation as an opportunity to build skills, knowledge or strengths is more likely to lead to stress-related growth. This is particularly pertinent for students; after all, study is very much an opportunity to build skills, knowledge and strengths. A key conclusion that she put forward is that if you choose to see stress as a positive factor, it can help create 'the biology of courage' that will help you grow through challenging situations (McGonigal, 2013, 6:30).

Perhaps stress is not as much of an enemy as we thought. As a student, if you can understand the positive potential of stress as you look to build skills, knowledge and strengths, it will be an important mindset to apply to your academic challenges.

The evidence that convinces me of the value of thinking about your attitude to stress

Ford and Wortmann (2013) wrote *Hijacked by your brain*, which considers the impact stress has on your brain. They came to similar conclusions to Kelly McGonigal, discussed in this statement:

> People who want to achieve peak performance optimize not only their bodies and their technical skills and knowledge, but also their minds. They are intuitively able to focus their thinking centers on both learning from their alarms (stress response) and communicating to their alarms that their thinking centers are in control. (Ford & Wortmann, 2013, p. 46)

Thoughts from my teacher

People often say they are stressed and use that word quite flippantly at times by associating it with things like being overly busy, having deadlines or not having enough time. However, stress is a highly individual experience that depends on specific psychological determinants to ignite a stress response in the brain and throughout the body. As noted in this chapter, eustress is not overly concerning in terms of getting things done and overall wellbeing, while distress is something to be avoided as much as possible. Distress often occurs when individuals face situations that are **n**ovel or **u**npredictable or **t**hreatening, or where an individual feels like they don't have control over the **s**ituation (which forms the acronym **NUTS**, an appropriate mnemonic to help you remember what causes stress; Nagel, 2012).

Worryingly, young people are more vulnerable than adults to the impact of stress due to the fact that their brains are in a state of developmental reconstruction and maturation. And while things such as good time management might help to avoid creating stress, there are a few simple things you can do to help when you are feeling distressed. It turns out that regular exercise, healthy eating, plenty of sleep and the fostering of positive social relationships can all counteract stress. Now those might seem rather simplistic, but Bruce McEwan (2002), perhaps the world's leading stress researcher, has identified the importance of each of those to alleviating stress and bringing the body and mind back to homeostasis (a stable and constant state). This is especially important when you consider that prolonged or chronic stress can result in long-term social, emotional and intellectual difficulties as well as actually changing structures in the brain. Therefore, if you think you are stressed, ensure you are doing as much as you can to exercise regularly, eat well, get plenty of sleep and hang out with friends.

A final word on the value of thinking about your attitude to stress

Next time you hear other students talking about being 'stressed', you will be a couple of steps ahead of them by understanding the key ideas that we have touched on in this chapter, including the stress-reducing role that simple steps including exercise, sleep, socialising and eating well can have. You can also employ a mindset that recognises that there is a positive level of stress – eustress – and understand that stressful situations can have positive outcomes. However, if you find that your learning is negatively impacted by distress, you should look for support.

References

Cassidy, T. (2019, February 27). Private school not the key to success as small-town country kid comes out on top. *ABC News*. https://www.abc.net.au/news/2019-02-27/alec-walsh-the-country-kid-who-topped-city-students-in-results/10850952

Ford, J., & Wortmann, J. (2013). *Hijacked by Your Brain: How to free yourself when stress takes over*. Sourcebooks.

McEwen, B. (with Lasley, E. N.). (2002). *The End of Stress as We Know It*. John Henry Press.

McGonigal, K. (2013, June). *How to make stress your friend* [Video]. TED Conferences. https://www.ted.com/talks/kelly_mcgonigal_how_to_make_stress_your_friend

Nagel, M. C. (2012). Stress and the mind of young people. *Generation Next*. https://www.generationnext.com.au/2012/05/stress-and-the-mind-of-young-people/

Nagel, M. C., & Scholes, L. (2016). *Understanding Development and Learning: Implications for Teaching*. Oxford University Press.

CHAPTER 2

The role of a growth mindset, grit and making hard choices

Nothing in the world can take the place of persistence. Talent will not; nothing is more common than unsuccessful men with talent. Genius will not; unrewarded genius is almost a proverb. Education will not; the world is full of educated derelicts. Persistence and determination alone are omnipotent. The slogan 'Press On!' has solved and always will solve the problems of the human race.

Calvin Coolidge, former president of the United States

The power of a growth mindset, grit and a framework for making hard choices

Perhaps the most important part of the journey as a learner is understanding that we have choices about the way we think about learning. Three models of deliberate thinking are presented in this chapter – a growth mindset (leaning into challenging work), grit (persevering toward long-term goals) and a framework for making hard choices (thinking about 'who am I to be' in our choices). Being deliberate in your thinking at important moments will add a positive dimension to your learning.

How to use a growth mindset, grit and a framework for making hard choices in your learning

If we have control over the mindset that we take into learning experiences, class time and study time, then what mindset should we be aiming for?

We start this discussion by looking at the research of Carol Dweck, Professor of Psychology at Stanford University. She has developed the ideas behind the 'growth mindset', the idea that with the right mindset we can improve our capacity.

The theory of the growth mindset stemmed from looking at how students dealt with challenges. Some students looked forward to challenge – 'I love a challenge,' they might say in response to difficult work. Other students would see difficult work as a likely step to failure – 'I am not good at this,' they might say (Dweck, 2016).

The first attitude, looking forward to challenging and difficult work with the confidence that you will be able to succeed and being prepared to persist with effort until you do, is a growth mindset. The second, being threatened by difficult work and assuming that you do not, and will not ever, have the ability to succeed at it, is a fixed mindset. ('I'm just not a maths person' is a common fixed mindset statement). It probably goes without saying that students with a growth mindset do better in the challenges they are confronted with, in areas as diverse as academics through to sporting and artistic endeavours. They do better not because they are inherently more talented, but rather because they believe in their ability to improve: they persist, they try different strategies and, with effort, they do improve (Dweck, 2016).

This brings us to the point where you can take action with your study and learning efforts. When you are confronted by something that challenges you in your learning, you now understand that your choice of mindset is going to influence the learning outcome. Backing yourself to be successful, trying different strategies and reminding yourself that persistence and challenge are what build capacity ('I love a challenge') will support the learning process.

The lesson from the theory of the growth mindset – to value hard work and even failure (because it is an opportunity to learn) and to understand that persisting with challenging work is what builds your capacity – is crucial for a learner. When you encounter something hard, or something that you have not achieved the first time, this becomes a crucial moment in your learning. This is a great chance to build your capacity through your persistence, through trying another approach and through remaining confident that with effort you will find a way.

Dweck's research is not that different from the insights and research of Angela Duckworth, Professor of Psychology at the University of Pennsylvania. Her observations stem from her time as a teacher, thinking about what makes students successful. She found that more important to student success than IQ or family background was a factor she called 'grit'. She describes grit as being 'passion and perseverance' for long-term goals, 'sticking with your future, day in, day out … and working really hard to make that future a reality' (Duckworth, 2013, 2:55). This is relatively easy for those students who have a strong focus on their long-term goals, perhaps a student who has always known that they want to be a doctor. For those students without a career focus, an understanding that strong grades, a strong base of learning and a strong work ethic will maximise future options is a good start. However, looking around for a long-term career goal that excites you, and that you want to work toward, will help.

Interestingly, Duckworth describes Dweck's growth mindset theory as being the best idea she has heard about building grit in people (2013). Put these two things together and I think that you have a choice as a learner. Are you going to buy into a growth mindset and value the fact that hard work, effort and perseverance will produce positive benefits? Are you going to understand the importance of grit in achieving success – really sticking with and working toward your long-term goals, day in and day out (more than just the night before an exam or assignment is due)?

The third mindset idea that I want to present to you is around making hard choices. As a student I suspect that you will face many tough choices around what to do with your time – are you going to sleep in until lunchtime on Sunday or get up and do some study? Go to a movie on the Saturday night before an exam block or fit in an extra revision session? In the third week of semester, will you follow through with your goal of updating your subject summaries or will you spend the time watching random videos on YouTube? The way you react to these hard choices will form an important part of your mindset.

Ruth Chang, a University of Oxford professor, provides an important insight into making hard choices. She describes hard choices in the following way: 'In a hard choice, one alternative is better in some ways, the other alternative is better in other ways, and neither is better than the other overall' (2014). Chang suggests that this becomes a choice between two options that are 'on par'. She emphasises that these choices don't have to be big, and I suspect that around study they will tend to be small choices that you have to make a number of times. A hard choice around study might be as simple as one of those proposed in the previous paragraph – the night before exams are you going to spend your night studying and sleeping well (a better option in one way because it will help position you to be successful with your exams) or will you have a late night socialising with friends (a better option in one way because it is likely to be more enjoyable)?

Chang tells us that the hard choices are a chance for us to stand behind an option, stating 'here is who I am' with this choice. In the case of the night before the exam, the person has the chance to say where they stand. For a person with a focus on doing well academically, it is likely that they will say that 'who I am' is someone who wants to be successful in exams. This doesn't mean that socialising with friends won't be the superior choice at other times. After all, socialising is part of having fun and managing stress as a student. But with this deliberate choice the exam preparation is prioritised for the long-term goal of being successful academically.

I find myself referring to this framework in making decisions regularly – I like to think of it as the 'who am I to be' challenge of hard choices. For example, I have a colleague who is happy to go for a run and a swim on Friday mornings. I have to wake up at 4.30 am to make it in time. However, because I want to get fitter (here is who I am in this hard choice), I choose to get up and go for the run, even though it is very early in the morning and I would like to get another 90 minutes of sleep.

The three models that we have discussed, growth mindset, grit and making hard choices, give you a framework for being more deliberate about your thinking and decision-making as a student.

The evidence that convinces me of the value of a growth mindset, grit and a framework for making hard choices

There is a compelling overlap between the researchers that we have looked at in this chapter. The collective summary of Carol Dweck, Ruth Chang and Angela Duckworth's work is that if we are conscious and thoughtful about elements of our mindset, including the deliberate way we make hard choices, the way we tackle challenging work and the way we persevere in our work toward hard goals, then we increase our chances of success, including in our endeavours as learners.

Thoughts from my teacher

Mindsets can have tremendous impact on your levels of motivation and, by association, your success in all that you undertake. The work of the individuals noted in this chapter is closely linked to decades of research related to self-efficacy beliefs. According to world-renowned psychologist Albert Bandura (1977), *self-efficacy* refers to an individual's belief in their capacity to act in ways necessary to produce specific performance goals. In simpler terms, self-efficacy refers to your confidence or self-belief in your competence or chances of successfully accomplishing a task and producing a favourable outcome.

Importantly, while aspects of confidence are innate and linked to personality traits, other aspects of this important mindset can be nurtured. For example, finding success in achieving small tasks or overcoming some obstacles through effort or perseverance can enhance self-efficacy beliefs. This can also be supported by observing the people around you, especially those you consider role models; seeing people similar to yourself succeed by sustained effort raises your own beliefs about also possessing the capabilities to master similar activities.

Finally, your emotional state can influence how you judge your self-efficacy. When you are feeling down, stressed, anxious or experiencing other negative emotions, you should work to find a positive outlook before engaging in new or challenging tasks. Positive emotions can literally boost confidence and, by association, self-efficacy beliefs. In the end, emotions and mindsets are inextricably linked and how you feel can directly affect how you perform in the short and long term.

A final word on a growth mindset, grit and a framework for making hard choices

Growth mindset, grit and hard choices provide us three thinking tools that will help us in our learning. Growth mindset encourages us to see the value in challenging work and to understand that remaining confident in our ability to master it through persistence will increase our chances of improvement. Grit reminds us of the importance of keeping long-term goals in mind and working toward them, and the hard choices framework challenges us to think about 'who am I to be' in the decision-making process when we feel conflicted between two options that both provide benefits.

References

Bandura, A. (1977). Self-efficacy: Toward a unifying theory of behavioral change. *Psychological Review*, *84*(2), 191–215. https://doi.org/10.1037/0033-295X.84.2.191

Chang, R. (2014, May). *How to make hard choices* [Video]. TED Conferences. https://www.ted.com/talks/ruth_chang_how_to_make_hard_choices

Duckworth, A. (2013, April). *Grit: The power of passion and perseverance* [Video]. TED Conferences. https://www.ted.com/talks/angela_lee_duckworth_grit_the_power_of_passion_and_perseverance

Dweck, C. S. (2016). *Mindset: The new psychology of success* (updated ed.). Ballantine Books.

CHAPTER 3

Remembering to do the things you love

> *The journey is the reward.*
> Chinese proverb

The power of doing the things you love

Setting academic goals is impressive. Giving them an appropriate priority in your life is important. However, there is value in maintaining balance while studying. Making time for the things that we enjoy will help us stay the journey with our study ambitions, as well as enjoy that journey more, keep us fit and help us manage the negative elements of stress.

How to keep doing the things you love as you study

In contemplating the challenges of study, it is possible that we come to a time when we decide that we need to knuckle down and focus on our work. Often part of this process is completing some sort of weekly planner to organise our study – a reasonable first step in managing our efforts. However, scheduling some enjoyable activities as well as our study makes it more likely that we will be able to stick with our study plan for longer.

Douglas Barton has worked with many students around how they approach their learning and studied what makes students successful (Mindshift, 2016). His observation is that students who cram their timetable full of study are not able to commit to their schedule and end up very quickly giving up, whereas those students who find a place in their schedule for enjoyable activities are able to stick to their timetables much better.

In a TEDxYouth talk, Barton identified some of the characteristics that differentiated top students from the rest (TEDx Talks, 2015). One characteristic that he highlighted was that when the top students came to timetable their weekly planner, they started by including non-study activities, like socialising, hobbies, sport and work. In contrast, most other students only included subjects and study tasks. He suggested that for the minority of students who included non-study activities, it meant that they had committed to doing things that they enjoyed, and this meant they were happy and balanced and more likely to commit to their timetable. He mentioned that most students are not able to stick to their timetable for even a relatively short time – for example, over 50 per cent of Year 11 students had abandoned their study planning within a week (TEDx Talks, 2015).

What we are talking about here is a lot more important than just the issue of sticking to a timetable for your study. A lot of students talk about the challenge of dealing with stress as a student. If you take the time to schedule activities that you enjoy, then you are also going to help manage stress. In Chapter 19 we look at the importance of exercise to brain health. Setting aside time for hobbies and interests that include physical activity will help maintain a healthy brain. Without fun, we are really assuming a 'grit your teeth' approach to study and that is going to be hard to maintain over any length of time. For a number of reasons, it makes sense to make sure that you keep finding time to include the things you love in your schedule.

The evidence that convinces me of the value of doing the things you love as you study

Alec Walsh was one of the top Year 12 students in Queensland in 2018. In fact, he was placed among the top 30 Year 12 students in Queensland despite what some might consider the relative challenge of studying at a country school, Kilcoy State High School (Cassidy, 2019). In discussing his success, he provides some great advice for other students. The secret to his success 'was not hour upon hour of tireless study, but rather organisation, relaxation and simply loving his school' (Cassidy, 2019, 'Secret to success, study not the answer' section). The article sought the expert opinion of Shelley Davidow, who said that the studies conducted by the HeartMath Institute in Florida over the last two decades have shown 'a distinct correlation between a calm and happy state of mind, high performance and low anxiety in students' (Cassidy, 2019, 'Teachers hold the key' section). Davidow says that 'too many teachers and parents give the "you need to be prepared, work really hard, have sleepless nights or you'll be flipping burgers the rest of your life" speech … And it's just not helpful, so when this man [Alec] says he loves his school, his teachers and took time to de-stress, they are all absolute prerequisites for thriving' (quoted in Cassidy, 2019, 'Teachers hold the key' section).

Thoughts from my teacher

Sometimes it can feel like your whole life is all about school! There are the pressures that your parents and teachers might place on you regarding school, assignments, homework, grades and other elements of your life. You might even put a lot of pressure on yourself! This can lead you to negative affective, or emotional, states and negative outcomes in terms of your overall wellbeing and educational outcomes. That is why it is always important to keep things in perspective and, as such, always keep in your mind that students only spend about 15 per cent of their week at school. They spend more time asleep, about 33 per cent. Students spend most of their time, however, at home, awake, mucking around, being with family and friends, and experiencing life. What students do with that time is so important given that there is a fairly substantive body of research noting that time spent doing the things that are liked and invoke passion have a positive impact on academic achievement. This is especially true when those things include physical activity. In his book *Spark: The revolutionary new science of exercise and the brain*, John J Ratey (2008) offers an extensive research-based narrative documenting how physical activity truly enhances the mind as well as the body. However, there are things beyond physical activity that you can do to separate your mind from school. In the end, you need to find what works best for you, but always remember that if all you do is focus on school, then you are unlikely to do as well as if you find other passions that clear your mind and provide respite for your brain.

A final word on doing the things you love as you study

Study is important, but by taking the time to make sure we keep in touch with hobbies, sport and social activities, not only do we enjoy ourselves more, but we put ourselves in a position where we are more likely to be successful with our study as well – a true win–win situation.

References

Cassidy, T. (2019, February 27). Private school not the key to success as small-town country kid comes out on top. *ABC News*. https://www.abc.net.au/news/2019-02-27/alec-walsh-the-country-kid-who-topped-city-students-in-results/10850952

Ratey, J. J. (with Hagerman, E.). (2008). *Spark: The revolutionary new science of exercise and the brain*. Little, Brown and Company.

MindShift. (2016, November 11). Three things top performing students know that their peers miss. *KQED*. https://www.kqed.org/mindshift/46951/three-things-top-performing-students-know-that-their-peers-miss

TEDx Talks. (2015, March 26). *What do top students do differently? | Douglas Barton TEDxYouth@Tallinn* | [Video]. YouTube. https://www.youtube.com/watch?v=Na8m4GPqA30

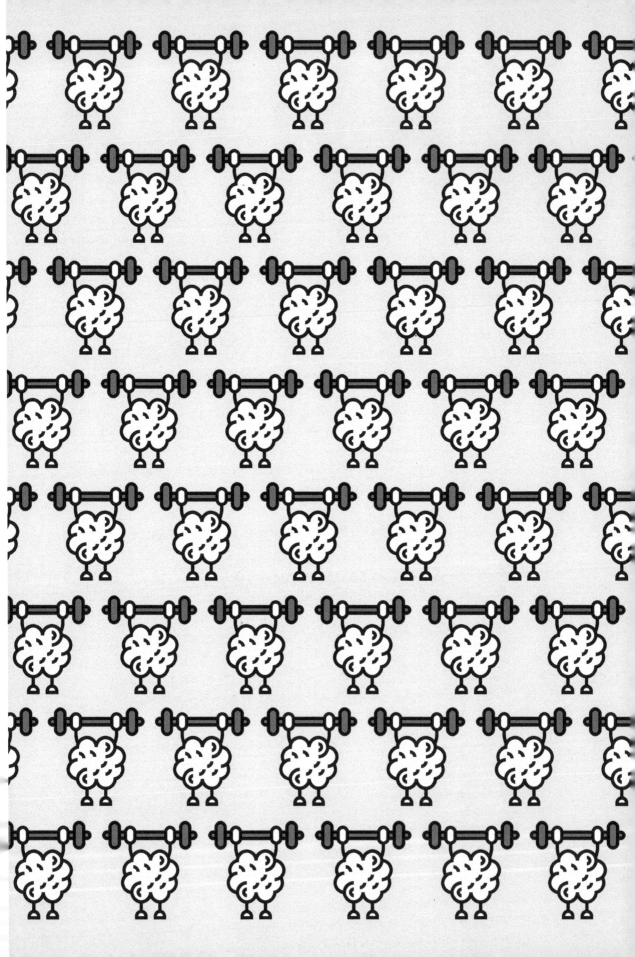

CHAPTER 4

Academic intensity

The time that leads to mastery is dependent on the intensity of our focus.
Robert Greene, *Mastery*

The power of academic intensity

Many people seem to measure a lot of what they do as a student by the hours spent – 'I spent six hours at the library working on my assignment until 11 pm' – rather than by how well they used that time. Indeed, the length of time spent on a task is sometimes worn as a badge of honour. Focusing instead on how much effort and intensity you are putting into your learning efforts, both during class time (subject classes, lectures and tutorials) and as you study, will ensure that you are getting the bang for your buck that you deserve.

How to make academic intensity work for you

I suspect that you have your own definition of the term *intensity*. In this case, I want to use the term in the context of how you approach your learning and study, to introduce an element of a learner's mindset that I think is needed to be successful – the commitment that you make to the task of learning. That is, the intensity with which you approach study.

Approaching a task with intensity is not something I promote as a characteristic solely of successful learners. My local professional men's basketball team is the Brisbane Bullets and I am lucky enough that the school basketball team I coach can go and watch them train from time to time. The intensity with which the players tackle every drill, from individual shooting to practice matches, is noticeably higher than when I watch a local club team train. I think this is a great example of the way we should be approaching learning – after all, both elite basketball and high-quality study share the common characteristics of setting goals, looking to improve, reflecting on performance and trying to get the most out of our efforts.

Back to the perspective of being a student, and from my observations and experiences, intensity means:

- making the most of the learning opportunities in class – being careful that your attention is on the task that potentially brings the greatest learning
- sitting down to study without distractions and pushing to work hard while studying
- starting early on revision and assignment tasks
- having clear goals toward which you are working, both in terms of individual subjects and overall study
- looking for opportunities for extra learning, including reading in the subject area beyond what is covered in class
- taking responsibility for your own learning, rather than relying on a teacher, parent or peer to push you
- seeking and learning from feedback wherever you can
- sitting in class where you are going to be able to learn well (the back row may not be the best answer) and sitting with people who do not distract you (be prepared to move away from friends who are talkative during class time) or, even better, will enhance your learning.

In understanding academic intensity, it is also important to understand the opposite of academic intensity, which is what I would describe as 'academic compliance'. Academic compliance is something that I see as being very common and something that I think most people will recognise. By academic compliance, I mean a student who is involved in the activities of learning but with little personal drive, passion or responsibility.

Students at the level of academic compliance generally remain on task during class. When there is a break in the lesson, they often choose to spend this time socialising. They do a fair job of completing their homework or compulsory tutorial assignments. When asked about their study, they complain about how long it takes them to complete relatively modest tasks, while admitting that they are also texting and using social media. Their results are satisfactory and they are happy to talk about how to improve things when pushed. They are even prepared to set goals if pushed by a teacher, tutor or parent. Assignment tasks are largely done in the 48 hours before the due date and most exam revision comprises of the time-honoured technique of 'cramming'. When assessment tasks are returned, their focus is on the mark rather than trying to learn from the feedback and looking for opportunities for improvement. These students are complying with everything that is asked of them but are unwilling to work independently to learn more deeply or extend their learning. Because of this, what they achieve for every hour they spend working in class or at home is significantly less than a student who works with intensity for the same period of time.

Here is a profound decision that you have to make – what level of intensity are you going to commit to your studies?

Many students who work at a level of academic compliance have worked at that level for many years and it may be a challenge to break those habits. During these students' early high-school years, their parents are likely quite supportive of their academically compliant attitude because they get acceptable marks from teachers (including for behaviour and effort), they sit down in front of some study each night (not particularly effectively), they don't get in trouble at school and at times they even seem to be working very hard (cramming and rushing last-minute work).

It is easy for academically compliant students and their parents to think that they are doing a good job, when they are, in fact, a long way behind those students showing genuine academic intensity.

A lack of academic intensity, both in the classroom and at home, is what holds many students back. The great news is that overcoming this problem does not take a huge commitment of time but rather a focus on getting the most out of your time. Indeed, some evidence suggests that students with a half-hearted approach to study can take up to three hours to complete one hour of work – committing to academic intensity while you study might actually save you time.

After all, if a class is scheduled to take 60 minutes, the length of time committed does not change regardless of how much effort you put in. What changes is the intensity of your effort and the amount that you get out of the class. Similarly, if you are going to sit down for 90 minutes to study, then that 90 minutes will pass. The only question is, are you going to work at the level of academic compliance and get a bit of work done? Or are you going to set yourself a higher standard and work with intensity, resulting in getting some quality work done?

Many of the chapters in this book deal with habits, skills and choices that will increase academic intensity. However, I think that just by making this concept of academic intensity one that you think about and make conscious decisions about, you are already building a successful mindset as a student.

So, let's think about what needs to happen if you are going to commit to working with academic intensity. The first thing to acknowledge is that the habit of working with intensity will take some time to build, especially if you have been happy in the zone of academic compliance for some time. You are going to have to be prepared to persist with the idea of academic intensity to change your habits. When you find yourself meandering through a study session with social media, or your attention wandering during class, you will need to challenge yourself, which leads to an important point about the transition to working with academic intensity.

If you have been working in the world of academic compliance, much of your motivation will have been extrinsic – reasonably good grades, happy parents, possibly even some recognition or awards for good results. To move to the next step, academic intensity, the focus is on being intrinsically motivated (looking to satisfy your own motivation for learning rather than relying on external influences to drive your behaviour) and satisfying your own higher standards (for example, getting the most out of your study time, thinking about your career goals or simply wanting to be a better educated, better informed citizen).

A simple way of building the habit of academic intensity and putting your own intrinsic focus on it, is to set small goals for each class or study session and then give yourself a quick ranking afterwards. A scale might look like this:

1. I worked with academic intensity for the whole session.

2. I generally worked with intensity, but I veered off task for short amounts of time.

3. I did a reasonable job, but I struggled to concentrate for most of the time and when I look back at my work, I can see that I have only made modest progress.

4. There was little true progress made in the time.

There is another element that I like around the language of compliance and intensity, or on this scale the first description versus the third description, and that is the subtlety of the language that links compliance to a bureaucratic level of achievement concerned with meeting minimum standards, whereas intensity is more closely linked with results characterised by excellence.

The evidence that convinces me about academic intensity

Life is far too interesting to spend it doing ineffective study. When students start to challenge themselves about the intensity behind their study efforts and value their time enough to say that they are either studying with intensity or not at all, those wasted periods of ineffective study are reduced.

Thoughts from my teacher

Intensity requires effort, concentration and focus. Too often, however, all three of these important components of intensity are negatively affected by distractions, with many students now living in an age of distraction. In fact, it may be the case that technology has created a generation of students 'wired' for distraction. A growing number of researchers (for example, Carrier et al., 2015; Courage et al., 2015; Twenge, 2017) have found that the lure of various screen technologies and their associated functions are particularly problematic for students when trying to focus on one thing. This is because the developing brains of children and teenagers can become more habituated to constantly switching tasks given the interactive nature of technology and are consequently less able to sustain attention.

Even as some parents, teachers and researchers express unease and concerns about the digital diets of the young people around them, efforts for using and engaging with technology are intensifying, thereby expanding the technological territory surrounding students at school and at home. This can have a negative impact on intensity and efficiency when it comes to studying. If you are in the habit of looking at your phone while studying, you will find that the time needed to complete a task grows considerably and your intensity, your level of concentration and engagement toward the task, diminishes markedly as your brain grows tired from switching from one thing to another and back again. To that end, and in an effort to promote constructive and intense studying, it is important to eliminate the distractions of devices and screens. When studying, turn off your phone, disengage notifications and only use the screen and medium you need, if needed at all. This will help to avoid distractions and improve your academic intensity.

A final word on academic intensity

If you have made the effort to get yourself to a class or find a place to settle into some study, value your time enough to make sure that you are working with intensity. Set some goals, reflect on your effort, think about your intrinsic motivation and be disciplined enough to get away from techno-distractions.

References

Carrier, L. M., Rosen, L. D., Cheever, N. A., & Lim, A. F. (2015). Causes, effects, and practicalities of everyday multitasking. *Developmental Review*, *35*, 64–78. https://doi.org/10.1016/j.dr.2014.12.005

Courage, M. L., Bakhtiar, A., Fitzpatrick, C., Kenny, S., & Brandeau, K. (2015). Growing up multitasking: The costs and benefits for cognitive development. *Developmental Review*, *35*, 5–41. https://doi.org/10.1016/j.dr.2014.12.002

Twenge, J. M. (2017). *iGen: Why today's super-connected kids are growing up less rebellious, more tolerant, less happy and completely unprepared for adulthood*. Atria Books.

CHAPTER 5

Motivation

Only I can change my life. No one can do it for me.
Carol Burnett, American actress

The power of motivation

A crucial element of your mindset is motivation. By thinking about motivation and taking responsibility for strategies that might boost your motivation toward your learning, you can be more effective than those students who wait in the hope that motivation will happen to them.

How to use motivation to enhance learning

It goes without saying that motivation will be an important part of your journey as a learner. Students often express frustration at a lack of motivation toward completing their schoolwork. The aim of this chapter is to help you understand a little more about motivation so you can use that knowledge to identify activities that might help increase your motivation. I hope that at times when you are feeling unmotivated you might be able to use this knowledge to nudge yourself into action.

One of the models that looks to describe motivation is self-determination theory, developed by Richard Ryan and Edward Deci (1985, 1991, 2008) from the University of Rochester. Self-determination theory states that a person's motivation can be positively affected by three elements:

- autonomy (the degree to which we feel that we get to choose our own actions)
- competence (the feeling that we are capable of doing what we need to)
- relatedness (the development of relationships with others; Standage et al., 2003).

I want to use these three elements, autonomy, competence and relatedness, to look at ways that we can find strategies that positively nudge our own motivation.

Self-determination theory – using autonomy as a motivator

Autonomy refers to having a high level of choice over what we do. Clearly there are some limits to autonomy in terms of your study; for example, you probably have a limited range of subjects to choose from as a high-school or university student. However, as you mature as a student, there is the opportunity to make more decisions about how and when to study, which increases your autonomy over your work. I want to suggest that there are three things that you can do to increase your sense of autonomy as a student, which will have a positive impact on your motivation. These are:

- using goals that you set yourself
- understanding the idea of intrinsic motivation
- being deliberate about your level of interest in what you are learning.

Let's start by talking about the goals you set for yourself. In Chapter 7 we look at goals, and particularly the positive role that goals play in motivation, making them important in the context of this discussion. Having goals that you plan, revisit and revise is a good source of motivation.

The second strategy within autonomy is to understand the difference between intrinsic and extrinsic motivation. Motivation can be discussed as intrinsic (coming from within) and extrinsic (external) motivation. An example of extrinsic motivation might be praise from your parents. An example of intrinsic motivation might be enjoying the thought of learning and mastering a new topic. The more powerful force is intrinsic motivation and this is the one that you can take responsibility for. Nagel and Scholes (2016) describe intrinsic motivation as the 'desire to engage in activities because they are interesting, enjoyable and challenging' (p. 193). If you can approach your studies with a sense of curiosity, looking for your motivation in the enjoyment, learning and interest in your study, you will be in a strong position.

The final element, similar to looking for intrinsic motivation, is the part of autonomy that links motivation to your attitude to what you are learning. Showing interest in the subject matter increases your motivation and learning, and it is your attitude that can increase your interest in a subject. If you can, take subjects that you find interesting and challenging, rather than subjects that you 'should' be doing because they are seen as the pathway that successful students take, or they are subjects that might have some status about them. Then take a little time to find the challenge, interest and value in the subject. English is a subject that some people struggle to see the value in – after all, what do you get from reading books or poetry and writing essay responses? However, the value of spending time building your skills in understanding a variety of texts, being able to communicate in different genres to different audiences and building general literacy skills will help in every subject that you study in the future, in every workplace that you go into and in your everyday life in roles as diverse as understanding media to responding to advertisements.

Nagel and Scholes (2016) emphasise that 'numerous studies demonstrate that the more autonomous a person's motivation is ... the more effort a person puts forth, the more positive a person's functioning, and the more positive a person's outcomes are in terms of learning, performance and achievement' (p. 195). The bottom line is that if you can find elements in your study that motivate you intrinsically, you will be in great shape!

Self-determination theory – using competence as a motivator

The focus of competence as a student is having the feeling that you are building the abilities, knowledge and capabilities you need to be successful over time. A large part of this is developing study habits that encourage this feeling of working with competence.

I want to suggest four strategies that can build motivation through a sense of competence:

- understanding and celebrating that you are learning and that you are increasing your competence over time
- working without distractions, allowing you to feel competent when you work with focus on a task
- blocking out time and breaking activities into smaller tasks, providing a plan to tackle and succeed at those tasks, building a sense of competence
- understanding attribution, allowing you to connect your results with your efforts so that you recognise that you can impact your results through your efforts.

Sometimes it pays to take a step back and see ourselves as a learner – noting how far we have come and the hurdles we have successfully jumped, and reflecting on the abilities, knowledge and capabilities that we have built over time. Taking intrinsic pride in recognising the way you are building your skills and knowledge will help with motivation – and recognising that efforts to 'go beyond' the average level of knowledge by applying yourself to your study and looking for diverse opportunities to learn will provide a sense of true competence, and deservedly so.

When students spend significant periods of time sitting down to study but feel as though they are not accomplishing much, it is a direct challenge to their sense of competence. There is little doubt in my mind that for most people the biggest challenge to quality study time is distractions. Distractions from social media. Distractions from email. Distractions from technology. We discuss this topic further in Chapter 20, but these distractions (or attempts to multitask) will significantly impair your ability to study and learn. Making the effort to study in an environment free of distractions will improve your quality of study, your amount of progress, your sense of competence and your levels of motivation.

Chapter 12 looks at attribution, or the way we explain why we failed or succeeded. If we are prepared to attribute success or failure to elements that we can control, like effort or the quality of study techniques we use, it is likely to be more motivating because we know that these are elements that we can change and therefore improve.

In Chapter 16 we look at the pomodoro technique, which matches short blocks of hard work (say 15–20 minutes at a time) with a task that needs completing, followed by a break and then another short block with another task. This provides a sense of competence as we can see tasks being ticked off and progress being made and, by working in manageable time blocks, we are not trying to push the limits of our ability to pay attention to a task.

Self-determination theory – using relatedness as a motivator

In the area of relatedness, I want to suggest two ventures that might impact motivation:

- looking to study in a social setting
- looking to build some relationships around the final destination of your study.

Chapter 18 looks at using the 'social brain' as a study strategy – meeting face-to-face with students who are also keen to do some work to tackle an academic challenge. As well as the motivational benefits of meeting face-to-face, there are also benefits in terms of the learning tasks that can be engaged in, including deep discussions and teaching content to each other.

While it is a little bit more of a stretch in terms of a link to relatedness, associating study with what you are planning on doing in the future also builds motivation. If you are at high school and want to study at university, making those goals more tangible by attending university open days builds a connection to that next goal. At university, being involved in opportunities for internships, lectures from industry professionals and career days helps refine your goals and makes the next career step more attainable. Many professional associations have student memberships – joining a professional association that is related to your work ambitions helps make that goal more substantial and continues to build your motivation.

The evidence that convinces me of the value of motivation

Vero and Puka (2017), in looking at the importance of motivation as part of the learning process, described it as 'the most important factor' that can be targeted to improve learning (p. 58). Being aware of motivation as part of the learning process and being prepared to take steps to positively influence your own motivation will help support your efforts as a learner.

Thoughts from my teacher 👨🏻‍🏫

Motivation is an important aspect of learning and most of what we do. Understanding motivation, however, is actually rather complex as there exist numerous theories about what drives one person to do something while another might completely avoid the same activity. Broadly defined, motivation is a person's internal instigation and direction that influences their behaviour, or, more simply, motivation is something that urges someone to do or achieve something. The word itself comes from the Latin root *movere*, meaning to set in motion. Motivation is influenced by a variety of factors including, but not limited to, family, culture, health and prior physical, social, emotional and environmental experiences (Nagel & Scholes, 2016). Motivation is also subject to influence from parents, family members, peers and teachers, and also influenced by ethnic and cultural backgrounds. From a neurological perspective, motivation is intimately linked with the brain's limbic system where emotions and memories are housed and processed (Nagel & Scholes, 2016). That being said, you don't need to be a neuroscientist to know that emotion and motivation are linked, but you do need to know that motivation is not an emotion per se but rather a process that links emotion to action. That process in itself can be driven by intrinsic or extrinsic factors.

Extrinsic motivation, as noted earlier, generally arises from outside incentives or consequences, usually in the form of rewards or the avoidance of punishment. People who act to gain a reward or avoid a punishment modify their behaviour as a result of being externally motivated. Intrinsic motivation, on the other hand, is derived from an innate desire to achieve a particular task or engagement in some form of personally meaningful activity. This type of motivation often emerges spontaneously out of an individual's need for competence, autonomy or relatedness, as noted earlier. Importantly, such needs are deeply psychological in nature and, as such, rather personal. In school, feelings of interest and enjoyment, for example, vary from student to student and activity to activity, but when students experience such feelings then motivation is exceptionally high. Indeed, so powerful is intrinsic motivation that a person can completely lose track of time or external events when they are deeply engaged in activities that elicit such motivation. Interestingly, athletes will refer to this type of motivation as being 'in the zone', while some psychologists have labelled such intense interest and focus as 'flow'.

The key for you, then, is to ensure you develop behaviours and habits that may allow for the best opportunity for flow to occur, and, like many other things discussed in this book, these include getting enough sleep, eating well, eliminating distractions and creating a positive study environment. You may not find everything you do in school of interest, but you can increase the likelihood of finding a reason, or sense of intrinsic motivation, for what you do by ensuring you do all you can to foster a positive environment and state of mind for studying, learning and academic success.

A final word on motivation

Thinking about how and what motivates you will help you nudge yourself into action when you are struggling to get work done. If you sit and wait for motivation to come to you, you could be waiting for a while, which will, ironically, be demotivating in itself.

References

Deci, E. L., & Ryan, R. M. (1985). *Intrinsic motivation and self-determination in human behavior*. Plenum.

Deci, E. L., & Ryan, R. M. (1991). A motivational approach to self:Integration in personality. In R. A. Dienstbier (Ed.), *Nebraska symposium on motivation: Perspectives on motivation* (pp. 237–288). University of Nebraska.

Deci, E. L., & Ryan, R. M. (2008). Self-determination theory: A macrotheory of human motivation, development, and health. *Canadian Psychology*, *49*(3), 182–185. https://doi.org/10.1037/a0012801

Nagel, M. C., & Scholes, L. (2016). *Understanding development and learning: Implications for teaching*. Oxford University Press.

Standage, M., Duda, J. L., & Ntoumanis, N. (2003). A model of contextual motivation in physical education: Using constructs from self-determination and achievement goal theories to predict physical activity intentions. *Journal of Educational Psychology*, *95*(1), 97–110. https://doi.org/10.1037/0022-0663.95.1.97

Vero, E., & Puka, E. (2017). The importance of motivation in an educational environment. *Formazione & Insegnamento*, *15*(1), 57–66.

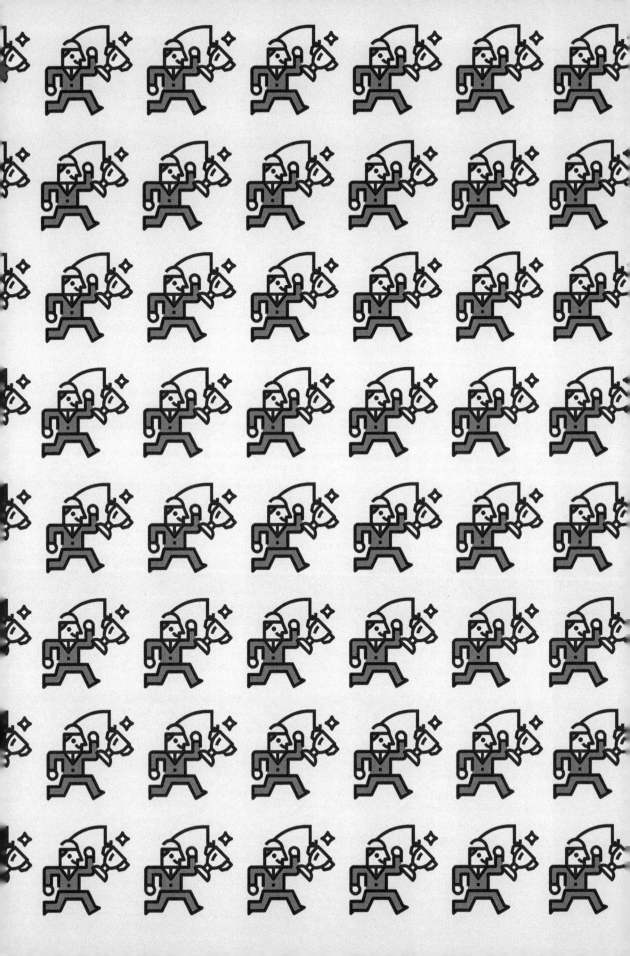

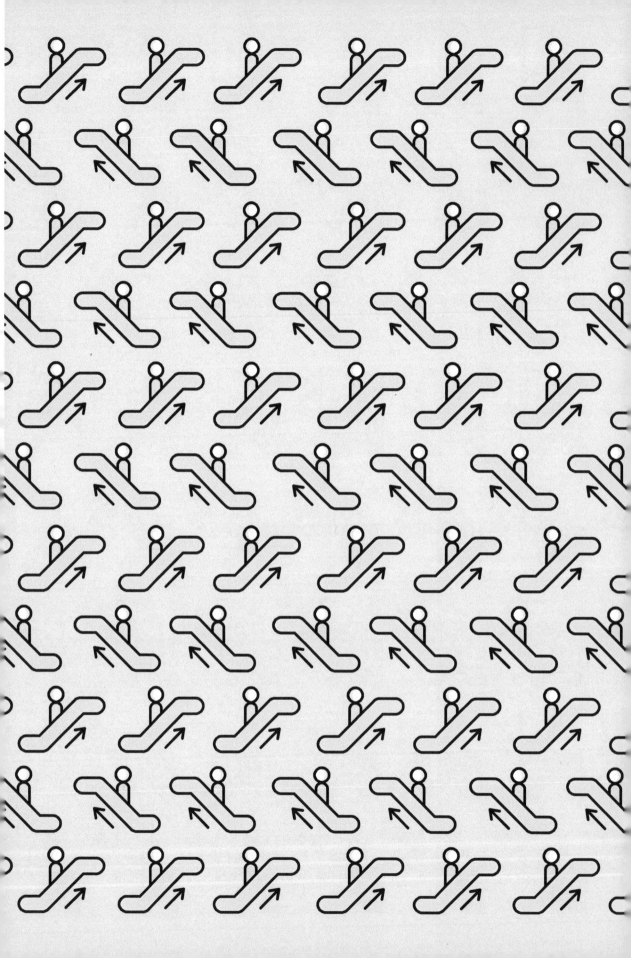

CHAPTER 6

Being engaged in class matters

*Life is like an escalator. You see, it carries you on regardless.
And you might as well enjoy the view and seize every
opportunity while you're passing. Otherwise, it'll be too late.*

Sophie Kinsella, *Twenties girl*

The power of being engaged in class

Your time in class is the most resource-rich time that you have to learn in, with teachers, lecturers, tutors, peers, textbooks and online resources all at your fingertips. Making the most of this time as your foundation for each subject means that even before you have to do any work at home, you have put yourself in a strong position to be successful.

How to get the most out of class time by being engaged

As much as this book is about study, I want to take you back to class for this chapter. This is because what happens in the classroom, tutorial or lecture matters, really matters, in terms of the results you get as a student. In terms of opportunities for learning, there is a strong argument that the classroom is the richest environment that there is. Linking back to the previous thoughts around academic intensity, you are there for the duration of the class, so you may as well maximise your learning over this time.

One of the rich experiences in a classroom environment is the ability to be around the questions asked in class. It does not matter if these are questions asked by the teacher or lecturer to check the learning of students, or by students looking for clarification to build their own understanding. Both are valuable.

Isidor Rabi won the Nobel Prize for Physics in 1944. In a *New York Times* article titled 'Izzy, did you ask a good question today?', Rabi discussed what he thought was the basis of his success as a learner. He put it down to the question his mother asked him after school each day: 'Did you ask a good question today?' (Sheff, 1988). Asking questions is one of the great, and unique, opportunities of the classroom, as well as listening and learning from the other questions that are asked and answers that are given.

Given this, I think that it is worthwhile to think about how well we, as learners, make use of the resource-rich environment of the classroom, tutorial or lecture. Let's think about the decisions that you make around class engagement, splitting the process into before class, during class and after class. The before-class steps that can be taken to maximise learning will include having all the resources needed for class, having completed any necessary preparation (homework, research, pre-reading), and being on time and in a state of mind that allows for learning. During-class steps will include sitting with people who are going to promote learning, restricting distractions such as phones, email and social media, participating when questions are asked and being prepared to ask a good question. After-class steps will require discipline to complete any notes, follow-up on any topics that were not finished and revise what was learnt to consolidate the learning from class.

The in-person learning experience is the foundation of learning efforts and being determined to make the most of it will be a strong start to building academic success.

The evidence that convinces me of the value of being engaged in class

The classroom has a number of subtle advantages over any other environment that makes it the core of learning, including being:

- the most resource-rich environment
- a buffer against many of the distractions that make learning less efficient
- a space with a common goal and purpose – learning about a topic led by a tutor, teacher or lecturer
- a space to work efficiently for a finite time which can significantly increase the return on your commitment.

Thoughts from my teacher

Too often people fail to understand that new buildings, well-decorated classrooms and the latest technologies are not the keys to a valuable learning experience. They help in some regards, but they are simply small facets of your education. Moreover, while teachers are far more important than those items just mentioned, they are also just a piece of the learning puzzle. You, the student, are also integral to your learning. That may sound naively simplistic, but many students know how to go through the motions of schooling and fail to seize the opportunity to fully engage with their learning. And while it is a truism that some subjects, and teachers for that matter, may be more interesting or inspiring, students also play a role in getting the most out of their learning.

The social dynamics of a classroom are unbelievably influential on learning and your individual contributions play a part in helping you to learn. This is becoming more apparent as universities are finding that more students drop out of online courses than those that require face-to-face interactions (Hil, 2012). It turns out that learning is a social endeavour and to get the most out of any learning environment means more than just showing up. Coming prepared, and with a mindset to participate, is perhaps one of the most significant things you can do to assist your learning; attuning to your learning environment, your teacher and your peers influences your outcomes. That may be one of the most important underlying messages in this book, as each chapter has been offered to assist you with making the most of your learning. What happens in class matters and how you prepare for and engage with that proposition will affect all aspects of your learning.

A final word on being engaged in class

You are in class anyway – be it a school lesson, a lecture or a tutorial. Choose to make the most of this time in the social endeavour of learning and you will build a great platform for your learning. Waste the time and you have still spent the same amount of time in class as an effective student, you will just get less out of it.

References

Hil, R. (2012). *Whackademia: An insider's account of the troubled university*. University of New South Wales Press.

Sheff, D. (1988, January 19). 'Izzy, did you ask a good question today?'. *The New York Times*. https://www.nytimes.com/1988/01/19/opinion/l-izzy-did-you-ask-a-good-question-today-712388.html

SECTION 2
Study techniques

CHAPTER 7

The value of setting goals

> *This one step – choosing a goal and sticking to it – changes everything.*
>
> Scott Reed, author

The power of setting goals

Goals are common in many high-performance environments – think sports, business and music – so why are they not used more to drive performance for students? After all, there is a significant body of research in this area led by researcher Edwin A Locke (for example, Locke & Latham, 2002), a United States-based professor who studied the impact of goals on performance in a variety of different scenarios. This research found that setting goals led to improved performance by those that took the time to consider and commit them to paper – and that improved performance is the power behind using goals to guide your efforts as a student.

How to set a goal as a student

One way that you can add more purpose to your study program is to take the time to write down and review your academic goals.

There could be a number of goals that you might set related to study. For example, you may set yourself the goal of studying with intensity for 90 minutes each evening for a whole term or semester. Or you might set yourself a goal to improve your results in a particular subject. Perhaps your goal might be more focused on your career aspirations – where you would like your study to lead.

A SMART goal provides a practical framework to do this. Each letter stands for an element in setting a goal. Using SMART goals is a commonly promoted strategy and the letters in SMART occasionally represent different things. However, if you start with a SMART goal that is Specific and Measurable, has Actions, is Realistic (and challenging) and contains a Timeframe, then you'll have set yourself a sophisticated and achievable goal to help guide your work and thinking.

Of course, while writing a goal is a great start, it is not enough in itself. An important question to consider is what we can do to help us succeed with our goals. Mark Murphy (2018), a researcher of the use of goals in workplaces, makes an important point about the value of writing it down to make goals stick, saying that the step of writing down a goal makes it 20–40 per cent more likely that you will achieve that goal. Another tool for accountability is telling someone your goals and having discussions about your progress. I would like to propose one addition to the SMART goal format to help build accountability, turning the SMART goal into a SMART'R goal, with the final *R* standing for Reflection. The reflection part of the SMART'R goal sets out the points in time when you are going to revisit the goal, consider how well you are sticking with your planned actions and look at any feedback you have received (maybe quizzes in class, a mid-semester assessment result or feedback from a teacher) to consider how you are progressing. Goals are not magical in themselves; they will require effort, revision and reflection along the way to consider your progress and make changes.

In the following table I have set out an example SMART goal (actually the new, improved SMART'R goal) – in this case to increase a mathematics mark from a C to a B over the course of a term.

Specific	Improve my maths mark from a C to a B for this term
Measurable	Term results at a B level or better
Actions	I will ask questions and listen to the other questions in each class so that I improve my understanding
	I will complete my homework each night
	I will revise the topics at the end of the third, sixth and ninth weeks
	I will search the internet for resources that fill any gaps in my understanding of the topics
Realistic (and challenging)	It is a goal that can be met and should be a good challenge
Timeframe	Complete over the term
Reflection	Review the goal every two weeks during the term
	Aggregate the feedback from each assessment task
	Review the goal at the end of the term

The evidence that convinces me of the value of setting goals

One of the foremost researchers on the impact of goals is Locke, who researched and wrote about the positive impacts that setting goals has on performance. His research, which is in part a summary of many research studies, provides evidence around the power of goals. Locke and Latham (2002) state that 'the effects of goal setting are very reliable ... specific, difficult goals have been shown to increase performance on well over 100 different tasks involving more than 40 000 participants in at least eight countries' (p. 714).

Angela Duckworth's discovery that goals were a significant driver of results for successful students from disadvantaged backgrounds is another piece of evidence that underpins the power of goals (2013). You might think back to Chapter 2, where I talked about Duckworth's discussions about long-term goals being part of grit – people working with determination toward their goals. This is another reminder of the importance of big goals. Perhaps when you think of study, the big goals are around a future career, so you can work toward those goals, day in and day out. Equally, setting a goal to get strong results so that you have as big a choice of career paths as possible might be a more general, big-picture goal to start with.

Thoughts from my teacher

The importance of setting goals cannot be underestimated in terms of learning outcomes. Goals and goal setting are linked to motivation and there is an abundance of research linking a student's personal values, objectives and goals with improved learning outcomes (see, for example, Dweck, 1986; Locke, 1996; Pintrich, 2000, 2003). It is significant to note that the type of goal you set helps to determine the extent to which that goal translates into some form of success or gain. The research suggests that your goals need to be specific and difficult but achievable (Larrick et al., 2009; Locke & Latham, 2006). For example, while doing your best and passing a test might be a laudable goal, getting a mark above 80 per cent or improving your score by 10 marks are better goals for improving your overall outcome. This is because the latter goals are precise and tell you exactly what you need to do to improve, while also providing a degree of difficulty that is more likely to require greater effort. Research tells us that as goals increase in difficulty and specificity, attention towards the task improves and performance increases in a linear fashion. Perhaps the most important thing to keep in mind is that goals can help you achieve what you would like to achieve as long as you plan them well and follow through to the best of your ability, which also means that you may, and should, alter your goals when needed.

A final word on goals

Using goals to focus your efforts and provide both a target to work towards and a structure for reviewing your work is a strategy that does not take a great deal of time, but does lead to improved performance. Of course, setting a goal is only the first step – you still need to be prepared to put in the work to make the goal happen.

References

Duckworth, A. (2013, April). *Grit: The power of passion and perseverance* [Video]. TED Conferences. https://www.ted.com/talks/angela_lee_duckworth_grit_the_power_of_passion_and_perseverance

Dweck, C. S. (1986). Motivational processes affecting learning. *American Psychologist*, *41*(10), 1040–1048. https://doi.org/10.1037/0003-066X.41.10.1040

Elias, M. J. (2014, August 27). SMART goal setting with your students. *Edutopia*. https://www.edutopia.org/blog/smart-goal-setting-with-students-maurice-elias

Larrick, R. P., Heath, C., & Wu, G. (2009). Goal-induced risk taking in negotiations and decision making. *Social Cognition*, *27*(3), 342–364. https://doi.org/10.1521/soco.2009.27.3.342

Locke, E. A. (1996). Motivation through conscious goal setting. *Applied and Preventative Psychology*, *5*(2), 117–124. https://doi.org/10.1016/S0962-1849(96)80005-9

Locke, E. A., & Latham, G. P. (2002). Building a practically useful theory of goal setting and task motivation: A 35-year odyssey. *American Psychologist*, *57*(9), 705–717. https://doi.org/10.1037/0003-066X.57.9.705

Locke, E. A., & Latham, G. P. (2006). New directions in goal-setting theory. *Current Directions in Psychological Science*, *15*(5), 265–268. https://doi.org/10.1111/j.1467-8721.2006.00449.x

Murphy, M. (2018, April 15). Neuroscience explains why you need to write down your goals if you actually want to achieve them. *Forbes*. https://www.forbes.com/sites/markmurphy/2018/04/15/neuroscience-explains-why-you-need-to-write-down-your-goals-if-you-actually-want-to-achieve-them/#48ed28927905

Pintrich, P. R. (2000). Multiple goals, multiple pathways: The role of goal orientation in learning and achievement. *Journal of Educational Psychology*, *92*(3), 544–555. https://doi.org/10.1037/0022-0663.92.3.544

Pintrich, P. R. (2003). Motivation and classroom learning. In I. B. Weiner, W. M. Reynolds, & G. E. Miller (Eds.), *Handbook of Psychology: Educational Psychology Vol. 7*, (pp. 103–122). John Wiley & Sons.

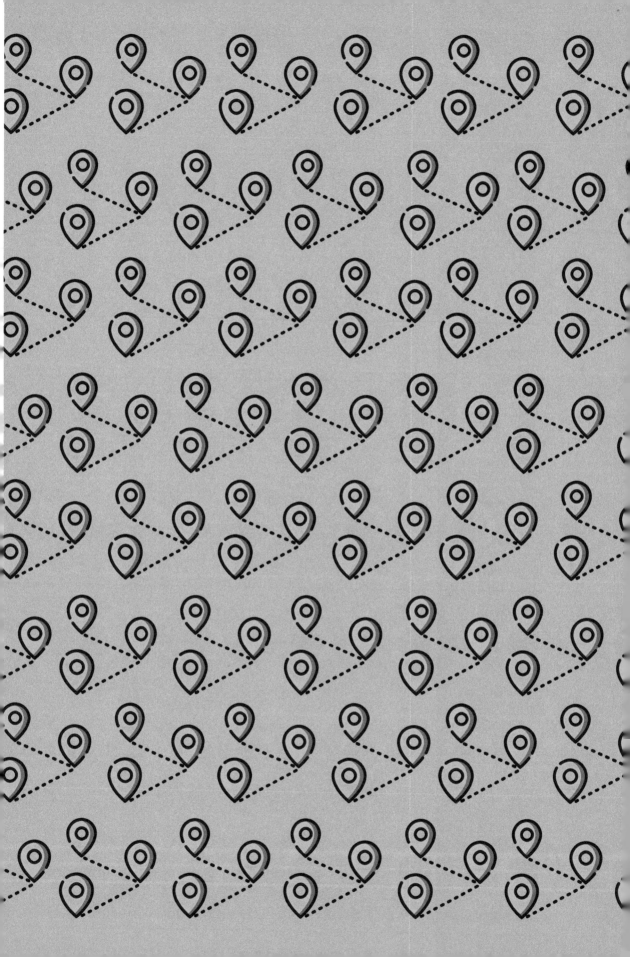

CHAPTER 8

Spaced practice (revision)

Practice only makes for improvement.
Les Brown, politician

The power of spaced practice (or distributed practice) as a study technique

Spaced practice is a fairly easy concept to sell on a cost–benefit basis. For the same amount of time that you are currently spending studying, research suggests that your marks could be 50 per cent higher just by spacing out this time into smaller, more regular blocks of study and revision (Carpenter et al., 2012). It is that easy. Rather than studying work as you learn it (homework) and the day before an exam (last-minute revision or cramming), spreading your study efforts to include some revision between when you learn something and when you are tested on it will improve your recall of the knowledge or skills learnt. In the long run, it will not take you any more time for improved marks, albeit with a little more discipline.

How to use spaced practice as part of your study

Basketball is my sport. I have done a bit of coaching and still play a little. I want to use a basketball analogy to further introduce to you the idea of spaced practice in a practical sense.

Let us consider a high-school basketballer getting ready for some basketball trials in eight weeks' time. I want you to think about your reaction if I, as a basketball coach, were to tell this young player that they should practise really hard for the next two days, then do nothing for seven-and-a-half weeks and then practise really hard for the two days before the trials. I think you would suggest that my advice was poor and I would agree with you.

However, is this not how we often behave as students? We learn something in a class or lecture, then we might do a couple of homework questions related to it, perhaps even summarise what we have learned, and then we don't do anything further with the information until just before the exam. This is an example of 'mass practice', practice at a couple of points of time and nothing else. As the opposite of mass practice, let's consider spaced practice with the example of learning something new, in this case maths and the topic of trigonometry. Rather than just learn and practise the concept when it is taught and then revise just before the exam, spaced practice would see you come back and do a few trigonometry revision questions, perhaps every two or three weeks. Each session does not need to take long and will increase the number of times that you are exposed to the knowledge and skills of trigonometry before the exam.

Let's look at this idea at a more practical and global level – how might spaced practice be applied to my study? Two key study tools that we will look at in later chapters fit very nicely with spaced practice: the use of a graphic organiser (perhaps a mind map or flow chart) and the writing and use of practice questions. Combined, these create a powerful study concept.

Firstly, what if every week you spent some time adding what you have covered that week to your graphic organiser and wrote some revision questions for that subject? Then, every three weeks you could also spend time reading back over the graphic organiser, answering the practice questions and following up on anything that you did not know. It would be a powerful way to combine the strategies of spaced practice, practice testing and the use of a graphic organiser.

A lack of time is a challenge for all students and I can see that by suggesting this as a study approach, I am adding another study activity that takes time. Indeed, a lack of time is almost universally the number-one challenge we hear students talking about. However, this review would not have to take a great deal of time: 20 minutes a week for a subject will be effective and it will save you time and stress cramming before the exam. In the research on spaced practice, students were not spending any extra time on their learning, but by spacing that time and revision they were able to get better results (Carpenter et al., 2012).

Looking at the bigger question of where the time for this strategy (or any other strategy for that matter) will come from, it can be an interesting exercise to set out a weekly planner and write in all your commitments – work, social, exercise, family and so on. Often, after mapping out their key commitments people find there is a little more time left for study than first expected.

The evidence that convinces me that using spaced revision is a powerful strategy

Educational Psychology Review published an article by Carpenter et al. (2012) entitled 'Using spacing to enhance diverse forms of learning' that looked at the impact of spacing as a study strategy. They quoted a number of studies that show significant improvement in student test results from using spaced revision. For example, one study that they cited looked at high-school students remembering history facts related to a course they had just finished. They were split into two groups: one who reviewed the content one week after finishing the course (immediate-review group) and the other who reviewed the content sixteen weeks after finishing the course (spaced-review group). Importantly, both groups spent the same amount of time with the content. Both groups were then tested nine months after finishing the course. Even though they had spent the same amount of time reviewing the content, the spaced-review group got a result 50 per cent higher than the immediate-review group. A tremendous result given that it took no extra time.

That same study also gave some important insight into the fact that there is no magic formula as to what spacing gap should be used, rather that revisiting material regularly over time led to better results (Carpenter et al., 2012).

Thoughts from my teacher

One of the most misguided notions around studying and learning is that of cramming before exams or assignments are due. You, your parents and probably most previous generations who attended school have been guilty of feverishly trying to cram as much information as you can into your head just before a test or deadline. The irony is that the memory systems of the brain do not operate most optimally when you do this. There is a vast amount of research that tells us that studying is most meaningful when it is spaced out, or distributed, over time (O'Donnell et al., 2016). Theories around distributed practice have been confirmed with empirical studies telling us that the most efficient way to learn a skill or remember information is to study or practise for shorter periods but spread out over several days or weeks. For example, studying a few spelling words each day for a week will ensure better outcomes than trying to master a large number of words bunched into one study session. It turns out that your memory systems function better when taking in small snippets of information over extended periods of time, which also allows for greater repetition and the consolidation of the information you are trying to learn. There is also ample evidence to suggest that studying the night before an exam is likely to lead to poorer results than studying over a longer period of time and leaving the night before the test as a time to relax (Brown et al., 2014). This, of course, means that you will also need to be organised and set aside time for your studies!

A final word on spaced practice as a study strategy

It is easy for me to go on about the case for using spaced practice in your study without acknowledging that it will take a level of commitment to execute this strategy. As you weigh up whether this strategy fits within the price that you are prepared to pay for the academic results you want, keep in mind that it is a strategy that will put you ahead of the vast majority of students who do a little when they learn something, a lot in the period before an exam and nothing else in between.

References

Brown, P. C., Roediger, H. L., III., & McDaniel, M. A. (2014). *Make It Stick: The Science of Successful Learning*. Harvard University Press.

Carpenter, S. K., Cepeda, N. J., Rohrer, D., Kang, S. H. K., & Pashler, H. (2012). Using Spacing to Enhance Diverse Forms of Learning: Review of Recent Research and Implications for Instruction. *Educational Psychology Review, 24*(3), 369–378. https://doi.org/10.1007/s10648-012-9205-z

O'Donnell, A. M., Dobozy, E., Bartlett, B., Nagel, M. C., Spooner-Lane, R., Youssef-Shalala, A., Reeve, J. M., & Smith J. K. (2016). *Educational Psychology* (2nd Australian Ed.). Wiley.

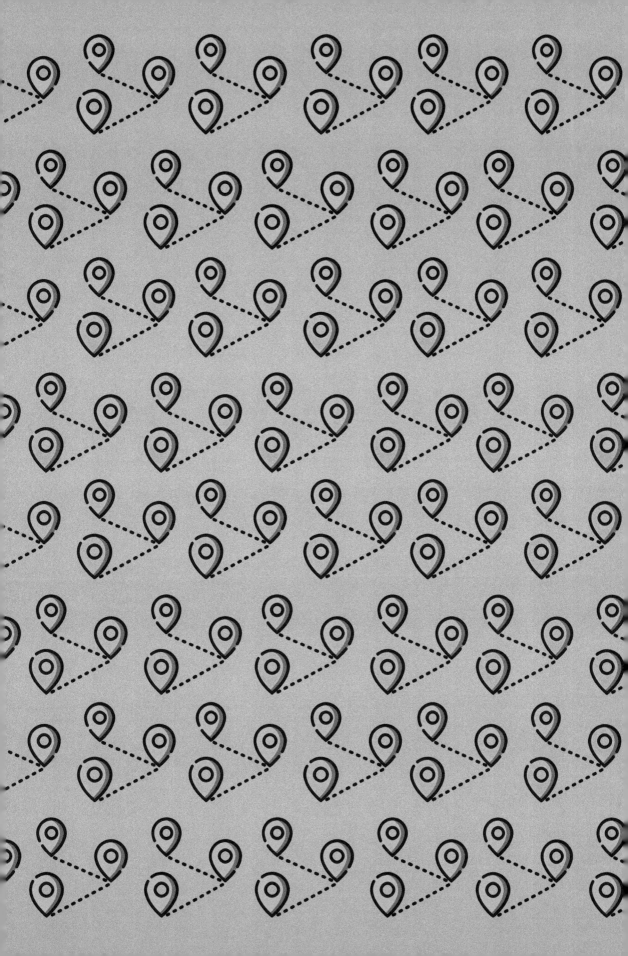

CHAPTER 9

Tackling assignments (and thinking about procrastination)

"

Procrastination is the art of keeping up with yesterday.
Don Marquis, author

"

The power of having a plan to tackle assignments

Having a plan to tackle assignments provides you with a threefold advantage. The first is that you are thinking about and building a process to overcome the challenge of procrastination. The second is that you are considering your learning and structuring a plan that allows you to be confident about the effectiveness of the steps you will take when you have to complete an assignment. You are also preparing a process that allows you to learn from the feedback given to you and improve.

How to build a plan to tackle assignments

There is a useful model that I have adapted to challenge procrastination in assignment writing. It comes from the punctuated equilibrium model (Gersick, 1991). The model is often used to describe the ways that groups work over time, achieving little in the first half of their time as a group, then becoming increasingly effective toward their deadline.

This is similar to how many students approach their assignment work, doing very little in the early weeks before starting to make some progress and then finishing in a last-minute rush. We know that this stands opposite to the approach that will bring the best results, which is to break the task into manageable components and work through these in an ordered fashion. Figure 1 on the following page shows two important models. The first shows an ideal plan of the progress of an assignment, in this case a research-style report (for other assignments the steps will vary, but the idea of breaking the task into components and working through them methodically still stands). The second shows my view of the way many assignments are currently approached, with very little progress in the early days and researching, drafting and writing occurring as the deadline draws near.

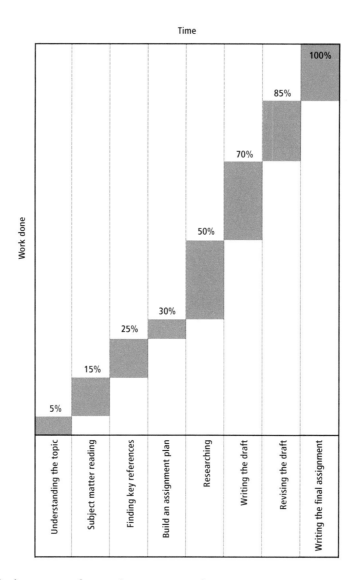

Figure 1a: Ideal progress of an assignment over time

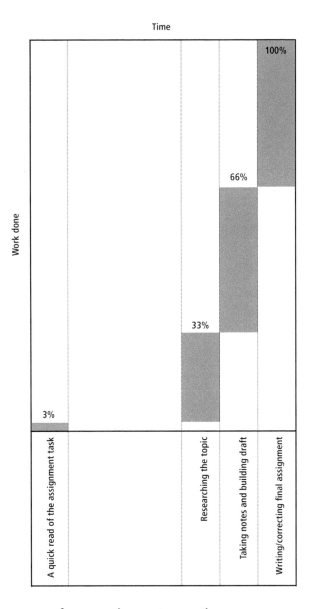

Figure 1b: Actual progress of many assignments over time

The challenge as a student is to decide whether you are prepared to make the effort so that your assignment progress looks more like the ideal plan. The key question I would pose around this discussion is: where will your assignment be halfway between the time the assignment is handed out and the task being due? Those students who have made thoughtful and measurable progress in the first half of the assignment timeframe are in great shape to complete an assignment that reflects their best work.

The model itself proposed the first part of my approach to completing assignment work – where will I be in my assignment by the midpoint between receiving my assignment and the due date? If I meet the challenge of having my work well developed by the halfway mark, then I know that I am in good shape and have beaten the punctuated equilibrium model.

One of the main challenges around completing assignments is procrastination. Webb (2016), a successful CEO and author, suggested a number of steps to help overcome procrastination, including:

- thinking ahead to the satisfaction of completing the task well (an intrinsically motivated way of thinking about the task)
- making a public commitment to the task (for example, telling a peer or family member)
- thinking about the cost of inaction
- breaking the task down into small pieces and focusing on completing a small task to start with
- finding a reward for progress.

These are some great strategies for beating procrastination.

The second major obstacle to good assignment writing is the lack of process and planning students put into building an assignment. It is surprising that the first thing many students do when beginning an assignment is to start writing, adding references and research as they progress. This leads to poorly communicated assignments that lack the depth of well-thought-out and carefully planned work.

The University of Queensland (n.d.) outlines a number of steps for completing successful assignments. The steps that they suggest are detailed following, while the comments in parentheses are mine. They provide some great structure for the process of completing an assignment – although every task will require different elements. A maths assignment, for example, might have significantly less research and more emphasis on designing a mathematical process and completing and recording calculations. Part of the challenge with different assignments will be identifying which steps need to be taken.

1. Topic analysis (including understanding the task sheet)
   - Brainstorming
   - Developing research questions (What is the focus of your research going to be?)
2. Researching and note taking
   - Reading critically (Is what I am reading useful? What is the value of each source? How can I use different sources to build the depth in my assignment?)
   - Taking notes for assignments

3. Planning your writing (including planning a structure that works with the word count)
4. Writing your assignment
5. Editing your assignment. (University of Queensland, n.d.)

I want to add one more step to this process: learning from the feedback given by the marker. Feedback is one of the most important inputs that teachers can provide to support student learning, and it follows that from a student perspective thinking about and responding to feedback is an important part of the process of learning and growing. When an assignment is returned it is very easy to be consumed by the mark, rather than learning from the feedback given by the marker. In Chapter 12 we look further at the importance of using feedback in our learning.

The evidence that convinces me of the importance of a process to tackle assignments

Webb (2016) summarises the challenge of procrastination:

> The problem is our brains are programmed to procrastinate. In general, we all tend to struggle with tasks that promise *future* upside in return for efforts we take *now* … So the short-term effort easily dominates the long-term upside in our minds – an example of something that behavioural scientists call *present bias*. (para. 2)

Procrastination is what dovetails into a last-minute assignment rush that has little thoughtful process about it, and is the key element that holds many students back from working to their full potential. Working with a process will help you combat the urge to procrastinate, particularly when you start to build confidence and see results that show that the process you use leads to higher quality work without the last-minute stress.

Thoughts from my teacher 👨‍🏫

Many people might think that the internet gave rise to procrastination, but people have struggled with putting things off for generations. Moreover, there is a long history of research suggesting that people who procrastinate have higher levels of stress and a lower overall sense of wellbeing; feelings of guilt for delaying work that needs to be done or worrying about deadlines due to leaving things until the last minute are not good for the mind or body (Sirois & Kitner, 2015; Tice & Baumeister, 2018). Importantly, procrastination can go beyond aspects of time management and reflect issues with self-regulation (managing various emotions) or having a poor concept of time linked to immature or reduced executive functioning of the frontal lobes. Fortunately, and in terms of meeting the timelines and demands of school, the brain is very plastic and there are some things that can help beat the procrastinating mind.

First, procrastination can be symptomatic of a fear of not succeeding, so try to find something positive about any task and make small specific steps towards the finish line – but most importantly, make a start! Second, when working on something minimise interruptions and distractions and use a timer to focus for set periods. In other words, put your phone someplace out of sight and mind and work for 20–30 minutes straight, then take a break. Third, if you find it difficult to avoid distractions, try implementing mechanisms that require you to make an effort to procrastinate … for example, having to log on to a separate device for social media or games. This makes you pause to think and reconsider the task at hand. And finally, reward yourself! Not only for completing the entire task but also for achieving small goals towards completion.

A final world on building a process to tackle assignments

If you can build an assignment process that allows you to get past the tendency to procrastinate, has you thinking strategically about the steps required to successfully complete each assignment and has you learning from the feedback given after the assignment, you will have a three-pronged approach to tackle any task with confidence.

References

Gersick, C. J. G. (1991). Revolutionary change theories: A mulitilevel exploration of the punctuated equilibrium paradigm. *The Academy of Management Review*, *16*(1) 10–36. https://doi.org/10.2307/258605

Sirois, F. M., & Kitner, R. (2015). Less adaptive or more maladaptive? A meta-analytic investigation of procrastination and coping. *European Journal of Personality*, *29*(4), 433–444. https://doi.org/10.1002/per.1985

Tice, D. M., & Baumeister, R. F. (2018). Longitudinal study of procrastination, performance, stress, and health: The costs and benefits of dawdling. *Psychological Science*, *8*(6), 454–458. https://doi.org/10.1111/j.1467-9280.1997.tb00460.x

University of Queensland. (n.d.). *Steps for writing assignments*. https://my.uq.edu.au/information-and-services/student-support/study-skills/assignment-writing/steps-writing-assignments

Webb, C. (2016, July 29). How to beat procrastination. *Harvard Business Review*. https://hbr.org/2016/07/how-to-beat-procrastination

CHAPTER 10

Exam routine: Building an exam technique

> *Every athlete acquires routines as a way to help control nerves.*
> Hope Solo, dual Olympic football gold medallist

The power of an exam routine

The quote that opens this chapter links routine with controlling nerves. In an academic context, exams are a potential source of nerves and anxiety. Building an exam routine of your own, that works for you, is a valuable addition to your study-skills toolkit. By doing this you will be in a better position to produce your best work in the added stress environment that is an exam. A routine will help you feel calm and prepared while facing the challenges of an exam.

How to build an exam routine

Just as two professional basketballers on the same team might differ with their pre-game routine, your exam routine will be something that will suit you. But while your exam routine will be personalised, there are a few common elements that are worth considering. Those are what you will do before the exam, during the exam and after the exam.

In Chapter 17 we discuss in more detail the role of sleep in learning, but it is relevant to mention here that sleeping well the night before helps academic effort the next day. This might be the start of your exam routine – a focus on at least a reasonable night's sleep the night before, which will give you a significant cognitive advantage compared to attempting an exam after an all-nighter. Your next step might be to make sure that you have all the equipment you will need. Searching for items at the last minute adds a level of stress that does not help academic performance. Your thinking might then turn to when you should arrive at the exam venue. Perhaps you like the sense of control that comes from arriving early and reading over your notes or completing some practice questions. These are all important aspects of ensuring your pre-exam routine sets you up for success.

A good pre-exam routine should also include some exercise. For me it was a 20-minute walk finishing about 10 minutes before the exam started. A brisk walk before an exam can help improve brain function, as shown in Figure 2 (the more colour in the image, the more brain activity, which will help in an exam), and provide some of the other benefits that we discuss in Chapter 19 including improved mood and concentration.

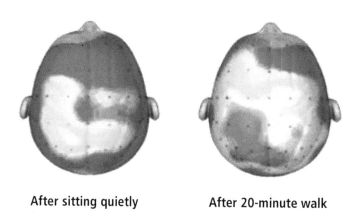

After sitting quietly   **After 20-minute walk**

Figure 2: Composite of 20 students' brains taking the same test
Source: From 'The effect of acute treadmill walking on cognitive control and academic achievement in preadolescent children', by C. H. Hillman, M. B. Pontifex, L. B. Raine, D. M. Castelli, E. E. Hall, & A. F. Kramer, 2009, *Neuroscience, 159*(3), p. 1050. Copyright 2009 IBRO. Published by Elsevier Ltd. All rights reserved. Used with permission.

You might want to set yourself some goals for the exam based on your experiences of previous exams. These goals might include working hard for the full period of the exam, reading the questions carefully, planning your time, planning your responses before writing or anything else unique to your situation or exam.

I want to finish with a slightly left-field suggestion that you might consider for your exam routine, especially if you find yourself getting nervous before an exam. University of Chicago researchers studied two groups of students (Harms, 2011). They asked one group of students to spend 10 minutes writing about their thoughts and feelings before an exam. Writing about thoughts and feelings was a psychological intervention that had been identified to reduce anxiety in other situations. The second group of students just did the exam without doing the writing. Those students who did the 10 minutes of writing performed better. They had a 5 per cent increase in accuracy in the final test compared to a pre-test, whereas the group without the writing had a 12 per cent drop in accuracy. Importantly, teenage students who reported usually being most stressed before exams showed the most improvement from doing the writing; they achieved a B+ average result compared to a B– for similar students who did not do the writing (Harms, 2011). For those who find themselves affected by worry and anxiety in exam situations, this is a strategy to try. Acknowledge and reflect on your feelings and you may be better equipped to overcome them.

The evidence that convinces me that an exam routine has value

There is an important link between an exam routine and research that looks at the idea of metacognition, or thinking about how we learn. Researchers at Stanford University split classes into two matched groups of students (Chen et al., 2017). For one group, a simple questionnaire was delivered to students a week before their test to encourage them to think about how they will approach their exam preparation and the resources they will use, in the researchers words making them more 'self-reflective' about how they would approach their upcoming exam. Those students receiving the questionnaire did better (by the difference between a B+ and an A–) in their exams and reported feeling less stressed by the experience of the exam (Chen et al., 2017). A lot of what is discussed in this book is about metacognition, thinking about how you learn, and building an exam routine that works for you is part of this process.

Thoughts from my teacher

Routine, routine, routine … this is not just important in terms of learning but also something the human brain thrives on! One of the common challenges associated with exams is anxiety. Many students will often become anxious during exam times and while some of that is due to the uncertainty of what may be on an exam itself, another factor contributing to exam anxiety is a sense of feeling underprepared. One way of alleviating such anxiety is through having a planned routine and using that routine consistently. It is significant to note that the brain is actually a patterning mechanism. Patterning refers to the meaningful organisation and categorisation of information, activities and experiences. When we develop patterns of behaviour, or what we might call routines, higher-order functioning is actually enhanced. This is likely due to the fact that routines provide a sense of security which helps to diminish feelings of anxiety and stress. The challenge, however, is finding a routine that works for you and sticking with it.

A final word on using an exam routine

It is normal to worry about how you'll go in an exam, but if you think about the power of having an exam routine that you know and trust, you'll get positive benefits from the confidence that gives you.

References

Chen, P., Chavez, O., Ong, D. C., & Gunderson, B. (2017). Strategic resource use for learning: A self-administeredn intervention that guides self-reflection on effective resource use enhances academic performance. *Psychological Science, 28*(6), 774–785. https://doi.org/10.1177/0956797617696456

Harms, W. (2011, January 13). Writing about worries eases anxiety and improves test performance. *UChicago News.* https://news.uchicago.edu/story/writing-about-worries-eases-anxiety-and-improves-test-performance

Hillman, C. H., Pontifex, M. B., Raine, L. B., Castelli, D. M., Hall, E. E., & Kramer, A. F. (2009). The effect of acute treadmill walking on cognitive control and academic achievement in preadolescent children. *Neuroscience, 159*(3), 1044–1054. https://doi.org/10.1016/j.neuroscience.2009.01.057

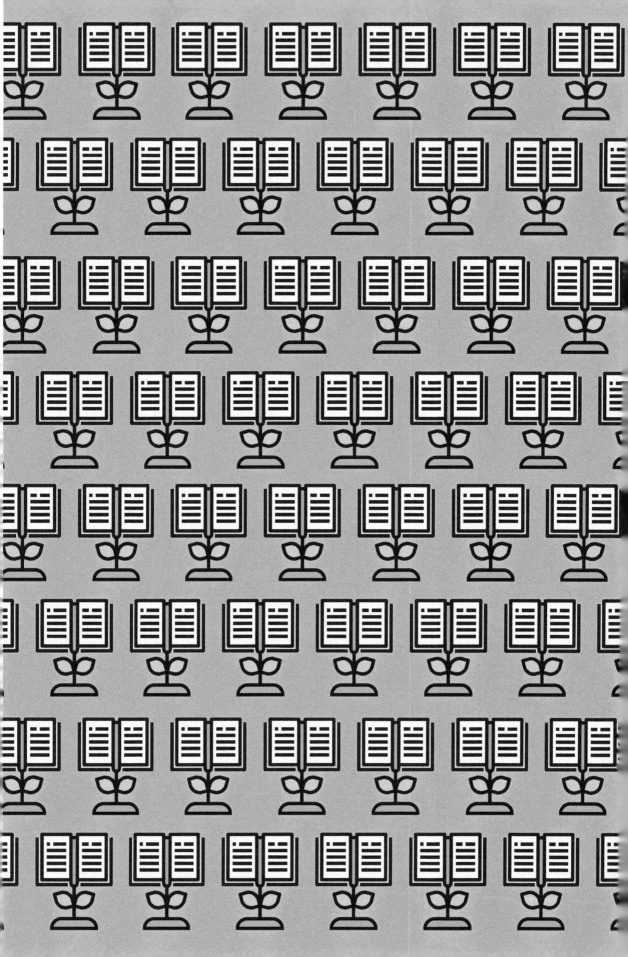

SECTION 3
Study skills

The basic activities that make up study: A beginning understanding of 'What is study?'

If it is important to you, you will find a way.
If not, you will find an excuse.

Unknown

The power of study

Every time that we come back into contact with knowledge (such as learning a list that we need to know for an exam) or skills (such as knowing how to calculate and graph a linear equation for maths), we are able to better recall the knowledge or perform the skills more confidently later on. This is the power of study – we want to put ourselves in the position that we become more and more confident with our recall of knowledge and ability to perform skills. This chapter establishes the basics of study, which we will build on with more sophisticated strategies in future chapters.

How to begin studying effectively

Students who have made a decision to improve their results often have trouble identifying exactly what to do. This is especially the case as people transition from primary school, where most of their work at home is set homework, to secondary school and university where students are meant to be working independently doing their own study. I often see students with a desire to improve, but uncertainty about what to do next.

There is often something mysterious about study and exactly what study is. The assumption is that the top students have some secret capacity and skills that set them apart in their pursuit of top grades – this is not true. There are many reasons why a student might be a top performer, but magic is not one of them. These students generally just work harder and more effectively. For example, in optional tutorials that I run for students it is almost always the top-performing students who attend – even though they already have a strong understanding of the work.

In the remainder of this chapter I want to unwind some of the mystery around study by setting out some tasks that will help make you an effective learner, as well as explain why studying makes a positive difference.

I propose that the three key aims of study are:

1. revising key material

2. summarising the most important elements of the information

3. checking that you know the information.

There has been a lot of research into how our memory works. It will not shock you to know that when we learn something new, we do a pretty good job of recalling it straight away but as time passes it becomes harder to recall (Jensen, 2008).

The key aim of study is to revisit the information and skills that we have learnt in class so that we remember the information and retain the ability to perform skills (for example creating a graph, building a spreadsheet or developing an essay argument).

This is the idea behind the first of the study aims – revising information so that we become better and better at recalling it or better and better at performing the skills we need. There are a number of practical ways that this can be achieved. Starting before class with a quick read of upcoming textbook chapters or articles will provide you with some exposure to the material before class. After class study tasks that focus on revising information to improve recall include re-reading notes, doing extra practice questions, reading (and re-reading) the relevant textbook chapter and making summaries of the work. Keep in mind that it is challenging tasks like doing practice questions that seem to be the most effective, because they force us to engage directly with the content and, in the case of practice questions, give us feedback on what we have learnt and what we are yet to learn.

The second element of study is to summarise the key information learnt. Let's say that you are studying for a legal studies exam, which might cover content across 50 pages of the textbook with 300 words per page. That leaves you trying to learn 15 000 words worth of content – a very big task. Equally, by the end of a university semester you are confronted with the daunting process of trying to gauge which information from a semester's worth of course content might feature in an exam. This is where the ability to summarise information is important. If you can distil that 15 000 words (using the legal studies example) into a more manageable set of notes, it now becomes much easier to re-read those notes when you come to revise them. Over the course of a semester, this process of summarising should be made easier by evaluating the content that is being emphasised in class and making notes as you go.

There is also evidence that suggests that we are more efficient at remembering images than words – and so the use of mind maps or flow charts is considered by many to be a powerful way of organising information (Marzano et al., 2001). Flow charts and mind maps are considered in more depth in Chapter 13.

The last of the three steps is checking that you know the information. This is best done through questioning – if I have an exam coming up on Australia's political history and want to learn the prime ministers of Australia, it is not until I ask myself to recite, or write down, the list from memory that I am testing whether I know the information well enough to recall it. This can identify gaps in knowledge that you can then focus on improving before the exam. Practice testing is important, and Chapter 14 is devoted to exploring this in more detail.

The evidence that convinces me of the power of study

The graph on the following page (Figure 3) shows the Ebbinghaus forgetting curve (1913). Ebbinghaus was a researcher who focused on learning about how memory worked. His work focused on the fact that when we are repeatedly exposed to information, not only does our immediate recall of the information increase, but also we tend to remember the information better and better over time. In Figure 3, each time the information is reviewed the retention of the information immediately increases, and the subsequent 'forgetting' of the information becomes slower.

While there are some criticisms of this model, at a general level it remains useful as it shows why we benefit when we revise material and skills. The more contact that we have with the information and skills, the longer we are able to retain that information. I suspect that a lot of times when we think about remembering information and skills, we assume that the endgame for a student is exams. Retaining knowledge and skills from subjects to help understand content in future study, and in future environments (including work), is also a valuable result of an effective approach to study.

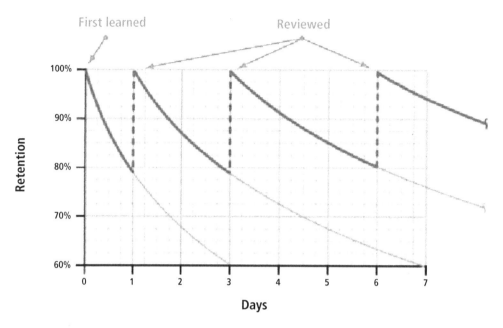

Figure 3: Typical forgetting curve for newly learned information

Source: From 'Ethical and unethical methods of plagiarism prevention in academic writing', by K. Bakhtiyari, H. Salehi, M. A. Embi, M. Shakiba, A. Zavvari, M. Shahbazi-Moghadam, N. A. Ebrahim, & M. Mohammadjafari, 2014, *International Education Studies*, *7*(7), p. 57. Used with permission.

Thoughts from my teacher 👨🏻‍🏫

The memory systems of the human brain are intriguingly complex and as yet not well understood. We do know that there are different types of memories and these are processed and stored in different ways. In terms of studying and recalling what has been learnt we also know that there are a couple of things that you can do to help this process. These tie into what this chapter has noted. The first of these are repetition and practice. This should not be surprising but productive repetition and practice go beyond simply repeating and require meaningful thinking. For example, you are more likely to remember the spelling of a new vocabulary word by exploring its meaning and writing it in a sentence to demonstrate its use rather than by simply writing it out a number of times. What you think about is what you remember given that memory is the residue of thought.

The second thing you can do to enhance your study habits is to overlearn, reflect and elaborate. This means to practise beyond mastery or revising what you have learned even if you think you have it down pat. Sometimes our memories play tricks on us and can be somewhat unreliable, so once you have studied and learned something, take the time to reflect and elaborate on it by rehearsing it in your mind or through notes or graphic organisers. Consider this to be hyper-reviewing and if you can establish this study habit you are more likely to remember all those things you need to know!

A final word on the activities that make up study

If you can find a process that allows you to revise key material learnt (and maybe even look at what is coming up before it is taught), summarise the most important elements of the information and check that you know the information, and you have the discipline to follow through on this process, you will be well on the path to becoming an effective learner.

References

Bakhtiyari, K., Salehi, H., Embi, M. A., Shakiba, M., Zavvari, A., Shahbazi-Moghadam, M., Ebrahim, N. A., & Mohammadjafari, M. (2014). Ethical and unethical methods of plagiarism prevention in academic writing. *International Education Studies*, *7*(7), pp. 52–62. https://doi.org/10.5539/ies.v7n7p52

Ebbinghaus, H. (1913). *Memory: A contribution to experimental psychology* (H. A. Ruger & C. E. Bussenius, Trans.). Teachers College Press.

Jensen, E. (2008). *Teaching with the brain in mind* (2nd ed.). Hawker Brownlow Education.

Marzano R. J., Pickering, D. J., & Pollock, J. E. (2001). *Classroom instruction that works: Research-based strategies for increasing student achievement*. Hawker Brownlow Education.

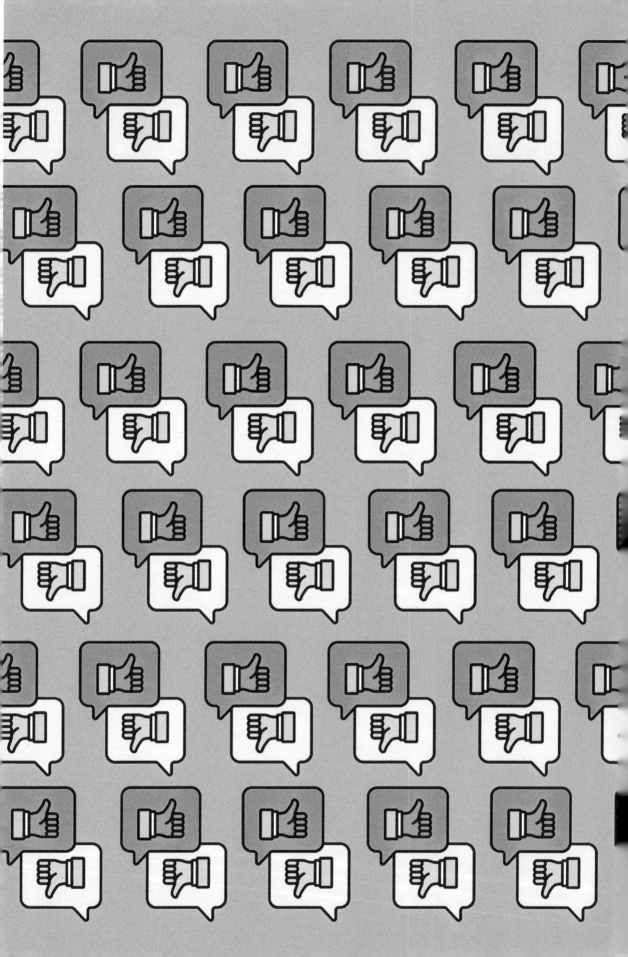

CHAPTER 12

The habit of 'attribution' and using feedback

If it is to be, it is up to me.
Phil Jauncey, sports psychologist

The power of using feedback

Do I have a deal for you – a study habit that, when mastered and enthusiastically applied, potentially makes a significant positive difference to your results and takes very little time. (I feel like this could be the start of an infomercial – but wait, there is more …)

The power of using feedback is that if you can take the time to harness the feedback that teachers, lecturers, tutors and peers are giving you, then you will be able to build a picture of the best way to keep improving. It is not easy, however. Very often when we get a task back the focus is on the mark alone, rather than looking for evidence about the things we have done well and the things we can improve on.

How to use feedback

An important part of using feedback has a fairly impressive name: attribution. This study skill comes from the research work of Weiner (1979). As fancy as the name *attribution* sounds, the concept is pretty simple. Attribution means attributing your work quality, both good and bad, to factors that you can control.

Let us consider a result that you might get, say a B in a maths exam. Attribution requires you to go back and look at the factors that you can control to work out where you might improve. For example, you can control your effort – did you put as much time into your work as was needed? You control your own behaviour in class – were you listening, engaging and asking questions in class? You control the way you undertake exams or assignments – did this process or routine work for you?

The opposite of attribution would be making excuses. Let's go back to that mark of a B in maths. If you decided that your lower-than-usual result was due to the fact that you do not like the teacher, there was noise in the classroom from construction and you had been sick the previous week, then you do not get the same amount of value from the feedback. These elements (the teacher, the noise, being previously ill) are all factors that you cannot control and do not teach you anything about your effort and learning.

I suspect that there will be some people who object and say that if you have had a bad teacher then surely you cannot be responsible for their influence on your results. The reality is that from time to time all students have teachers (and lecturers) that they do not get along with. There are plenty of other resources available for learning including textbooks, class notes, peers and online resources. The most successful students will continue to take responsibility for their learning and find ways to succeed.

Attribution is not only looking at the controllable things that you can improve but also wanting to give yourself credit for the things you have done well, to recognise them and keep doing them! If you explain away your success by saying 'It was an easy test', think about what you did to make it an easy test.

Closely related to attribution is feedback. Teachers understand that one of the key things they can do to improve your learning is to provide high-quality feedback. It follows that your job as a student will be easier if you are listening to teacher and peer feedback wherever you can. This includes when revision questions are being done (How does the teacher answer practice questions?), when students are reading out or answering questions (Which responses does the teacher really like? What characteristics of answers do they emphasise?), when there are opportunities for group work or peer marking in class and when assessment tasks are being handed back.

You might be thinking that you can see a bit of a link between the idea of a growth mindset and attribution, and I would be inclined to agree. Both work from the same idea that with persistence and a thoughtful approach, we are all capable of improvement.

Spending time thinking about all feedback and attributing results (both informal and formal) to your own efforts will not take much time but will, when sustained as a strategy, help to improve results. To go the extra mile, keeping a journal where you track feedback is a powerful plan. Recording the feedback forces you to think about it and having your feedback in one place allows you to quickly revisit previous lessons.

The evidence that convinces me of the importance of attribution and feedback

Hattie et al. (1996) looked at a variety of studies into learning to consider which study skills most affected learning. They found that teaching students about attribution, and encouraging them to use it in their practice, had an effect size of 1 – more than twice the effect size of the 0.4 threshold for a strategy that is often considered to be 'effective'. It would seem to be a powerful strategy, with the added benefit that it is not time consuming to implement.

Thoughts from my teacher

Success is in the eye of the beholder! As alluded to in this chapter, 'attribution theory is a psychological concept about how people explain the causes of an event or behaviour' (Smith, 2016, para. 1). In schools, students often experience 'desirable and undesirable outcomes (such as success and failure)' and then attribute the cause of those successes or failures to something specific, which in turn can affect motivation (Smith, 2016, para. 2). One of the biggest challenges with attributions is that they do not always accurately represent reality. For example, you might attribute failure to stable factors such as intelligence when, in reality, the failure was caused by an unstable factor like lack of effort (Smith, 2016). Unstable factors are those things that fluctuate, and you can therefore control, while stable factors are those things beyond your control. The important thing here is that the reasons you choose for your successes or failures can have a significant impact on your future performance, and that is why you need to pay attention to the feedback you receive. If you view success or failure as a product of luck, good or bad teaching, or other external factors, you are less likely to be motivated to do well. In this sense, feedback provides a platform for you to work on things such as effort or other mechanisms that you can control. In the end feedback and attributes work hand-in-hand to shape your vision of success.

A final word on the importance of attribution and feedback

When we step back and think about the topic of feedback more broadly it becomes evident that we grow from using feedback, from the time we were young and learned through feedback that touching boiling water was unpleasant and tripping while trying to go too quickly down the stairs hurt. Looking for and embracing feedback related to your academic tasks and reflecting on your own efforts will help you improve as a learner, especially as you start to build up a picture of the tasks that you do well and can be confident in, and the elements of your work that you can improve.

References

Hattie, J., Biggs, J., & Purdie, N. (1996). Effects of learning skills interventions on student learning: A meta-analysis. *Review of Educational Research*, *66*(2), 99–136. https://doi.org/10.3102/00346543066002099

Smith, M. (2016). Applying attribution theory to the classroom. *Psych(ed)*. https://psychologyineducation.wordpress.com/2016/09/11/applying-attribution-theory-to-the-classroom/

Weiner, B. (1979). A theory of motivation for some classroom experiences. *Journal of Educational Psychology*, *71*(1), 3–25. https://doi.org/10.1037/0022-0663.71.1.3

CHAPTER 13

Graphic organisers

*All you need is the plan, the road map,
and the courage to press on to your destination.*
Earl Nightingale, radio announcer and author

The power of a graphic organiser

Using a graphic organiser, what you might know as a flow chart or a mind map (let's refer to them as mind maps in this chapter), allows you to organise information in a way that makes it easier to recall, easier to find linkages between topics and easier to identify the most important elements learned.

How to use a graphic organiser to enhance learning

Most students will have used a mind map before; if not, a quick online search will provide plenty of examples. The traditional structure begins with the core topic in the centre of a page, with major concepts stemming from this core topic and other ideas branching from those concepts.

Figure 4 on the next page shows a very simple mind map that summarises the key topics in this book.

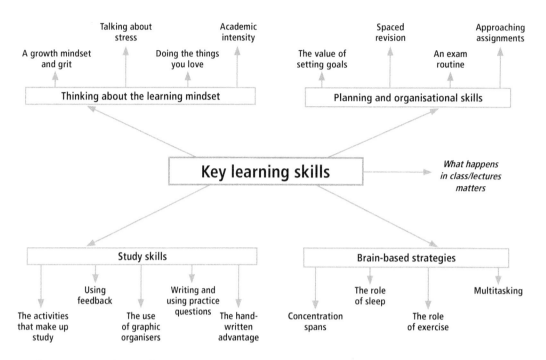

Figure 4: Sample mind map

The first question might be, why do mind maps work? There are many different answers: that they represent information as a picture and it is easier for the brain to remember pictures; that it forces us to organise and prioritise information within the mind map; or that looking at information visually helps us see important links between the information, which makes it a more sophisticated way of displaying and remembering information.

To provide an example of how a mind map might help us find connections between topics, let's build a little more on the mind map of the different chapters of this book, looking at some connections we might find around the topic of exercise. Exercise is important in managing stress, it might be important in students having fun and the immediate benefits of exercise (enhanced concentration and mood, for example) can be very useful when getting ready to sit an exam or to break up study into shorter efforts more suited to our fairly short concentration span. In the following diagram, the orange lines, and text in italics, now add this information to the flow chart, giving us a more sophisticated understanding of exercise and its impact on learning.

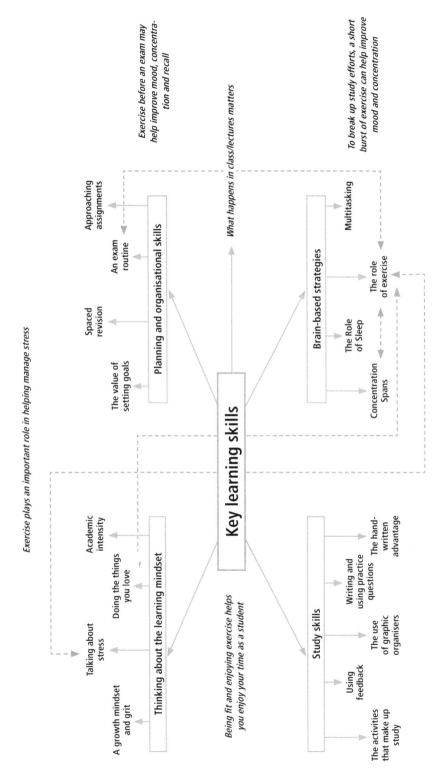

Figure 5: Building on the sample mind map

Indeed, the process of building a mind map forces the learner to sift through what information is important and what is not, summarise the key ideas in their own words and find connections between topics. By processing the information in this way, they are already more likely to recall it. From a memory perspective, there is a significant amount of information displayed in a mind map, usually with far fewer words than the equivalent block of text. This makes it an excellent resource on your learning journey.

The second question might be, when would I use a mind map? Here are a few instances where you might use a mind map:

- When you are looking to summarise a term or semester's worth of work. Start building a mind map early in the teaching period and consistently add to it so that all the information is on one page. At a practical level, do this by putting a piece of paper into the first page of your book and add the topics as they are covered.

- When planning an assignment. Start with the assignment topic in the middle, followed by the key sections and then the content that is added into the key sections. As you think of more ideas, or links between ideas, add them into your assignment plan. This is a great way to ensure that recommendations and conclusions are consistent with the discussion in the body of the assignment.

- Any time that a summary needs to be done. For example, if you need to summarise a number of pages of a textbook.

Part of the discipline of a mind map is that it is a finite document (the size of the piece of paper). By limiting the space available, you are forced to identify the most important information. This mind map will become one of the key revision materials in the hours leading into an exam. If you understand the ideas within a well-thought-out mind map, you can be confident that you have the key information that you need heading into the exam.

There are great computer programs that can create flow charts and mind maps for you. You may prefer to create them by hand. In Chapter 15 we look at the growing body of research that suggests that computer note taking is less effective than note taking by hand. Building a mind map by hand allows much greater freedom to make links and connections between ideas, and add further annotations.

The evidence that convinces me of the value of graphic organisers

Many educational theorists have confirmed the value of graphic organisers in improving learning outcomes. Marzano et al.(2001) considered 100 educational studies and from them distilled nine strategies that led to improved student performance; one of the top nine they identified was the use of graphic organisers, associated with a 27 per cent improvement in learning.

Thoughts from my teacher 👨‍🏫

As a visual aid, a mind map is a great tool for studying and consolidating learning. One of the great things about mind maps is that you can personalise the map by using colour schemes, letters and symbols that have some value to you and as such create a clearer association of your learning. Mind maps are also a great example of how our memory systems work better through visual representations, as they fire up greater neural connections and regions of the brain and engage them in a fuller capacity in comparison with simple text. Images can be powerful enough that they can stay within your grasp of memory for a very long time while you likely have to read text several times until you can remember much of it. This has been demonstrated in many studies. For example, in 2008 researchers found that students in Year 8 who used mind maps showed significant gains in conceptual and practical understanding on science achievement tests than those students who only took notes (Abi-El-Mona & Adb-El-Khalick). Moreover, in a sense, mind maps mimic the brain's architecture and thought processes in that they use multilateral thinking, going in many directions at once in a holistic manner, unlike the sequential processes of a computer, which mirror simple note taking.

A final word on graphic organisers

The great thing about using a mind map or flow chart is that there is no extra time cost involved. It provides you with a simple and efficient way of building a visual representation of information that will improve your understanding and recall of topics, which, after all, is the cornerstone of effective learning.

References

Abi-El-Mona, I., & Adb-El-Khalick, F. (2008). The influence of mind mapping on eighth graders' science achievement. *School Science and Mathematics, 108*(7), 298–312. https://doi.org/10.1111/j.1949-8594.2008.tb17843.x

Marzano R. J., Pickering, D. J., & Pollock, J. E. (2001). *Classroom instruction that works: Research-based strategies for increasing student achievement.* Hawker Brownlow Education.

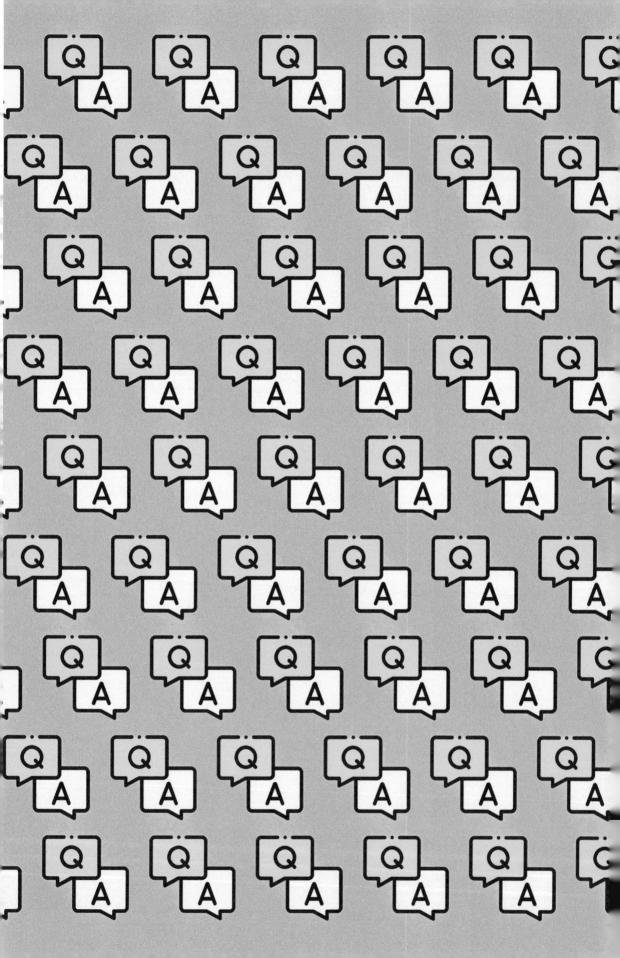

CHAPTER 14

Writing and using practice questions

Practice does not make perfect. Only perfect practice makes perfect.

Vince Lombardi, NFL coach

The power of writing and using practice questions

There are many revision strategies that remind us of the content that we have covered – reading notes, making summaries or highlighting important sections of work. None of these offer the power of testing ourselves. When we use practice questions, not only are we revising content, we are also demonstrating to ourselves what we know (the questions we get correct), and what we need to work on, all while replicating and practising for the exam situation.

How to write and use practice questions to enhance learning

The question of what to do with your study time is a crucial one. This chapter contains a well-researched and effective piece of study advice. Write yourself revision questions, or use revision questions that already exist, and test yourself using them.

There are multiple sources of practice questions available to you, including those that your lecturer or teacher gives to you, within your textbook, and from practice exams and past exams. If there are practice questions available, then use them. It is always better if you have answers that you can check your responses against, because knowing whether you are correct or not is a big part of the effectiveness of this study strategy. If you do not have answers available, it is your job to check that your answers are correct – cross-checking your answer with your notes, textbook or peers.

If there are no practice questions available, after going through all the potential sources, that gives you the interesting task of writing your own. This forces you to think hard about the most important topics that you have covered, the types of questions that you might be asked on an exam and the appropriate answers. There is no point in trying to create a shortcut here by writing easy questions that will be of no use to you. You need to anticipate as best you can the content and style of questions and create questions around that so that you are prepared for the exam.

A great strategy would be to write out some practice questions at the same time as you summarise information in a graphic organiser over the course of a term or semester, and then revisit these practice questions as part of your spaced revision.

One important characteristic of a practice test is that it should give you feedback on what you know and what you do not know. If your study is to just read over a textbook chapter, you really do not know what you will be able to recall during an exam. If you ask yourself practice questions, you know exactly what you do know and exactly what you have to put more effort into learning.

Another benefit of using practice questions is that it directs our focus to thinking about what might be on an exam, encouraging us to think about what topics are most important and what format the exam questions might take (elements that are not thought about if our study is based around re-reading texts and highlighted notes).

Douglas Barton spent years working with high-school students in a number of countries, considering what it is that top students do differently (TEDx Talks, 2015). He identified that the top students use practice questions to test themselves as part of their approach to their study. His comment on this technique:

> One of the factors in particular we found to be multiple times more effective (than IQ) to predict academic performance … was practice exams. We found the top students do more practice exams than anyone else. We found you can almost perfectly estimate a student's results by looking at the number of practice exams they've done. And we also found that we could almost perfectly rank a class from first all the way down to last just given the amount of practice exams they would do across a year. (TEDx Talks, 2015, 3:39)

The evidence that convinces me of the value of writing and using practice questions

Dunlosky et al. (2013) looked at a volume of existing research into the effectiveness of ten different study techniques, including highlighting, practice testing, spaced practice (they called it 'distributive practice'), re-reading and summarising. They rated strategies as high, moderate or low utility. Only two of the ten strategies were categorised as high utility: spaced practice and practice testing. A summary from Dunlosky et al. (2013) related to practice testing is:

> On the basis of the evidence described, we rate practice testing as having high utility. Testing effects have been demonstrated across an impressive range of practice-test formats, kinds of material, learner ages, outcome measures, and retention intervals. Thus, practice testing has broad applicability. Practice testing is not particularly time intensive relative to other techniques, and it can be implemented with minimal training. (p. 35)

Figure 6 highlights the results from a study that showed two groups of students taking one of two approaches to learning a text they had seen the week before, either re-studying a section of text or completing some practice questions about the text (Dunlosky et al. 2013). A week later they took a final test on the material. Over three experiments that the researcher used that varied the extent to which test questions moved away from the original context, practice testing produced significantly better results than re-studying (Butler, 2010; Dunlosky et al. 2013).

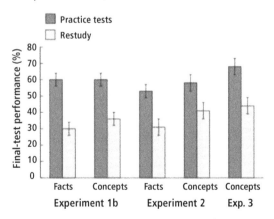

Figure 6: Accuracy on final tests that consisted of inference-based transfer questions tapping key facts or concepts, administered one week after a learning session that involved either practice tests or re-study, in Butler (2010). Error bars represent standard errors

Source: From 'Improving students' learning with effective learning techniques: Promising directions from cognitive and educational psychology', by J. Dunlosky, K. A. Rawson, E. J. Marsh, M. J. Nathan, & D. T. Willingham, 2013, *Psychological Science in the Public Interest, 14*(1), p. 33. Copyright 2013 SAGE Publications. Used with permission.

These results are not isolated – there is a significant body of research that supports testing yourself with practice questions as a very effective study technique (Butler, 2010; Dunlosky et al. 2013).

Thoughts from my teacher 👨🏻‍🏫

A major goal for teachers is helping students master new content and then helping those students develop strategies for long-term retention and retrieval of that material (He & Canty, 2013). For students, learning new material and consolidating that learning with previous material is an important aspect of doing well at school … and while this may seem fairly obvious, too often the methods for achieving mastery of content are not undertaken effectively. For example, simply reading through material or cramming for an exam are often over-utilised at the expense of activities that consolidate content. Always remember that:

Memory + Attention = Learning

And while teachers may employ different strategies to reinforce learning, including assignments, exams, quizzes, self-evaluation and analysis, practice questions appear to be one of the best mechanisms for learning (He & Canty, 2013). As the information in this chapter explains, taking time to work on prescribed questions, or forming your own questions as you go and then answering them, is one of the best ways to remember important content. Interestingly, numerous studies have also shown that when students take tests on studied material, it results in better retention and learning than additional studying of the target material, suggesting that using practice questions to test oneself would be useful in the retaining and retrieval of what has been learned (He & Canty, 2013). It is also noteworthy that in all domains of learning, developing levels of expertise or mastery of content occurs only with major investments of time. Practice questions offer a mechanism for positive investments in such time with a great degree of efficacy that transcends many other approaches to studying.

A final word on writing and using revision questions

When we sit down and spend valuable time studying, we want to choose the most effective practices that we can. Testing yourself with practice questions is a highly effective study practice, allowing you to revise your material while also giving you feedback on what you know well and what you need to work on.

References

Butler, A. C. (2010). Repeated testing produces superior transfer of learning relative to repeated studying. *Journal of Experimental Psychology: Learning, Memory, and Cognition, 36*(5), 1118–1133. https://doi.org/10.1037/a0019902

Dunlosky, J., Rawson, K. A., Marsh, E. J., Nathan, M. J., & Willingham, D. T. (2013). Improving students' learning with effective learning techniques: Promising directions from cognitive and educational psychology. *Psychological Science in the Public Interest, 14*(1), 4–58. https://doi.org/10.1177/1529100612453266

He, X. & Canty, A. (2013). A comparison of the efficacy of test-driven learning versus self-assessment learning. *The Journal of Chiropractic Education, 27*(2), 110–115. https://doi.org/10.7899/JCE-13-6

TEDx Talks. (2015, March 26). *What do top students do differently? | Douglas Barton TEDxYouth@Tallinn* | [Video]. YouTube. https://www.youtube.com/watch?v=Na8m4GPqA30

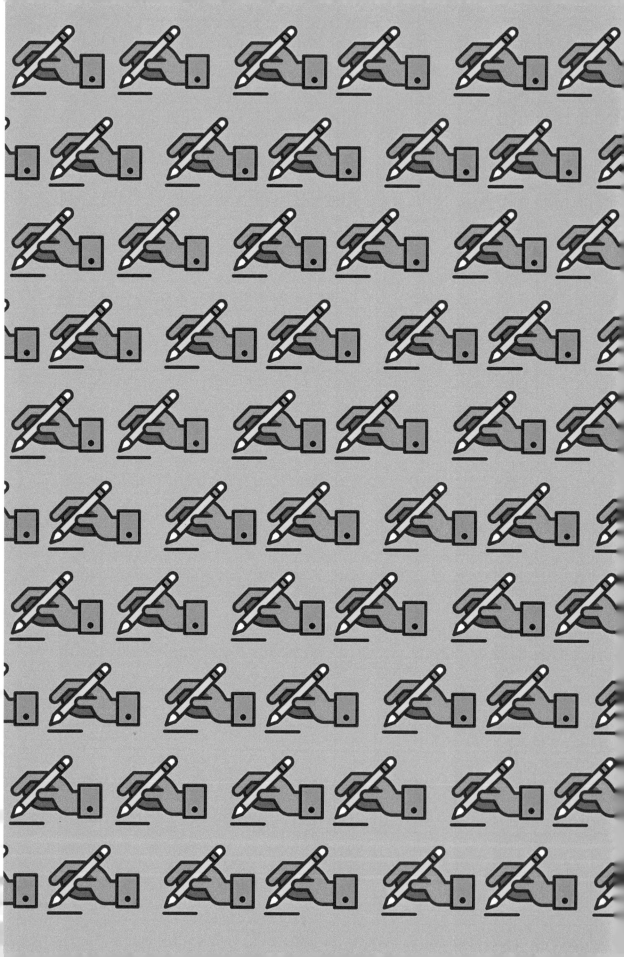

CHAPTER 15

The handwritten advantage

Handwriting enables civilization.
Toba Beta, *Master of stupidity*

The power of using handwriting

It is simple: if you handwrite your notes and revision summaries, there is evidence that you will recall that information better.

How to use handwriting for your study

Given that handwriting versus typing is a fairly simple concept, it may seem strange that I have dedicated an entire chapter to it. However, as there is evidence that note taking with a pen and paper leads to better recall of information, and recall of information is a key endgame of study, I think it is well worth thinking about. It may take a little more effort; however, that is the core of academic intensity – putting in a little more effort when it is rewarded with better academic outcomes.

There seem to be two points of advantage that research suggests you gain from handwriting your notes and summaries. Mueller and Oppenheimer (2014) set these out in their research, with the first advantage being a very practical one – there are reduced distractions while handwriting notes. There are no incoming emails, social media notifications or cat videos that provide distraction while using a notebook and pen. This theme of the potential cost of distractions has been a significant one throughout the book.

The second advantage comes from the fact that there seems to be greater processing of information when handwritten notes are taken. Notes taken by hand showed more evidence of summarising information, highlighting key information and finding links between information, whereas computer note takers tended to take down everything that was said. Interestingly, Mueller and Oppenheimer (2014) identified that the computer-based note takers had more words in total written down, but the point of taking notes is not the amount of content, rather the ability to summarise content. They characterised the computer-based notes as having shallower processing – tending more to rewriting what had been said.

A key academic skill is to pick out the most important information to be learned and handwritten note taking seems to support this. That does not mean that you should throw away the laptop as a note-taking tool completely. If you are aware of the computer-based note-taking shortcomings, it may be possible to overcome them. We all know how to close the emails and get rid of social media distractions while using the computer. We can also build a computer note-taking process that encourages us to summarise (use lists and diagrams to take down notes where possible), emphasise (highlight or bold key text) and process (conduct a five-minute review at the end of a class) the information from a class or a lecture. That said, Mueller and Oppenheimer (2014) warn that this is not easy; even with encouragement to do otherwise, computer note takers tended to keep on writing things verbatim, rather than processing and summarising the information.

Give handwriting a go. If you feel that you prefer computer note taking, then focus on building higher-quality computer notes rather than just writing down all of the content. Whether you are taking handwritten notes or computer notes, a focus on summarising efficiently, emphasising key points and finding connections between content will help your learning.

The evidence that convinces me of the value of handwriting notes and summaries

Mueller and Oppenheimer (2014) summarised their research clearly: 'On multiple college campuses, using both immediate and delayed testing across several content areas, we found that participants using laptops were more inclined to take verbatim notes than participants who wrote longhand (handwriting), thus hurting learning' (p. 1166).

Thoughts from my teacher 👨🏻‍🏫

For many students, the thought of handwriting notes compared to typing seems counterintuitive in terms of speed and efficiency. However, while the use of computers in schools has been available for a couple of decades, the evolution of the human brain has taken much longer and, as such, adapting learning to a technology-based environment is not as seamless as you might think. For example, taking notes by hand actually requires different cognitive processes than using a computer for note taking, and these processes have consequences for learning. Because writing by hand is slower, and perhaps seems more cumbersome resulting in not everything being recorded, it actually means that we tend to listen, digest and summarise information more succinctly and accurately. Taking notes by hand appears to ask the brain to do some heavy mental lifting and as such the effort associated with handwritten note taking fosters better comprehension and retention. Alternatively, you can type notes faster and perhaps transcribe what you see or hear word for word, but you do so without giving much thought to the content. Handwriting may not allow you to get every word down verbatim, but in comparison to typing it would appear that less is actually more in terms of understanding and learning.

A final word on the handwritten advantage

Handwriting notes rather than typing them is a relatively low-time-cost strategy, that fits well with the concept of academic intensity, and seems to be effective in improving learning – so make the effort to find a pen and paper and make the most of your time in class by processing the content into useful notes.

References

Mueller, P. A., & Oppenheimer, D. M. (2014). The pen is mightier than the keyboard: Advantages of longhand over laptop note taking. *Psychological Science*, *25*(6), 1159–1168. https://doi.org/10.1177/0956797614524581

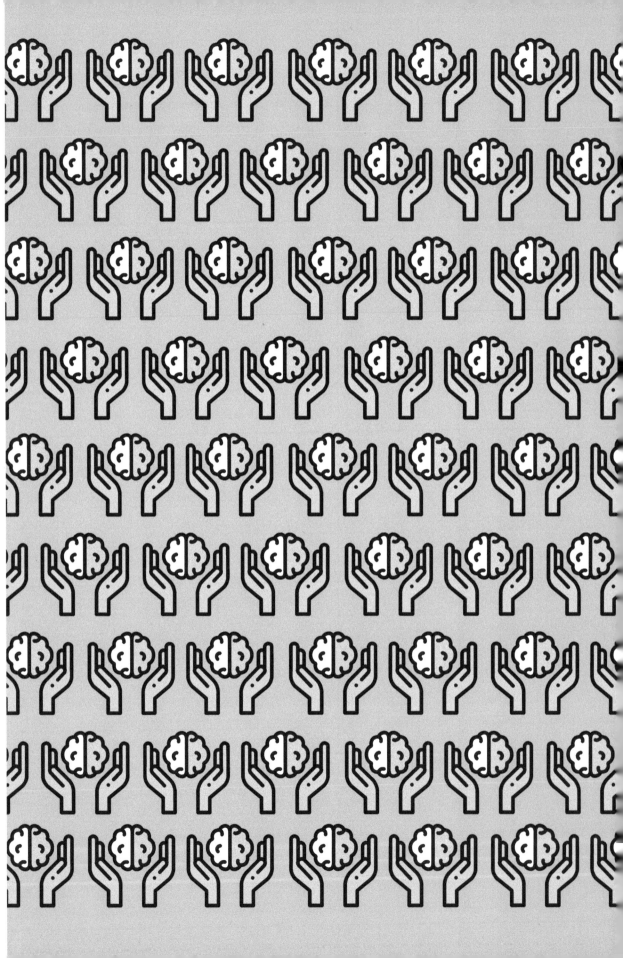

SECTION 4
Working with your brain

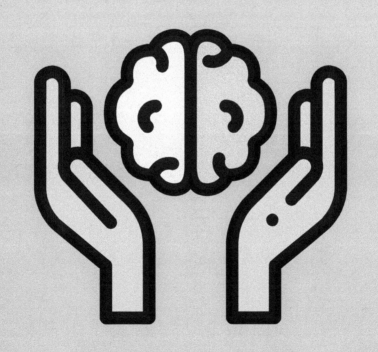

CHAPTER 16

Attention spans

Concentration and mental toughness are the margins of victory.
Bill Russell, NBA basketballer

The power of understanding attention spans

For many students the start of each semester is a time of some optimism. Goals are set, plans are made and good intentions are running high. However, like New Year's resolutions, many good scholarly intentions and new study habits do not last through the first month. One key issue is that students try to sit down and study for several hours every night, which does not match our ability to pay attention to a topic. Understanding the way attention works allows us to plan a study approach that is more likely to succeed.

How to use an understanding of attention spans to help your study

Trying to study for two or three hours on end, particularly in the evening when our brain has already done a full day of work, is problematic. Jensen (2008) suggests that our ability to focus on a task might be limited to 20 minutes, or even less. Rather than thinking about finding two- or three-hour blocks of study, focus on building a schedule that comprises of 15–25-minute blocks of deliberate and intense work, alongside regular study breaks.

There are a few strategies that jump to mind as I think about how to manage study time around a 20-minute concentration span:

- Aim to complete 20 minutes of hard work when you get home from classes or lectures – and be 20 minutes ahead of where you usually would be without going beyond your concentration limits (this is a personal favourite of mine, and I often find the 20 minutes of intended work morphs into 45 minutes of high-quality work).

- Start with the subjects you least like first – get them out of the way so you are working with your preferred subjects when focusing becomes a little more challenging.
- Take breaks – exercise is a great tool to break up your study time and helps improve your mood and focus.
- Move between subjects to break up what you are working on, creating some variety in your work and changing your concentration from subject to subject.
- Use the pomodoro technique. The pomodoro technique suggests using set time blocks for tasks (25 minutes), with a five-minute break between blocks, and a bigger break (20 minutes) after four blocks of work. There are plenty of apps that help with this timing.

Life is too good to spend it doing bad study. Using these techniques helps us adopt the idea of academic intensity that we discussed in Chapter 4, making the most of our time when we are studying.

You will undoubtedly personalise your study endeavours to match your attention span. Have realistic expectations about what you can do and think about how you can organise your study plans to work with, rather than against, your capacity to pay attention.

The evidence that convinces me of our limited attention spans

Memon (2019) outlined the reasons she thinks a pomodoro approach works well:

- Short breaks help you concentrate and fight boredom.
- Alternating work and breaks helps fight boredom.
- Taking breaks helps keep your decision-making ability sharp.
- A shorter period of work time makes you less inclined to try multitasking, which reduces effectiveness – there is a finite period of time and a set task, making it easier to stick to.
- It encourages you to 'chunk' your work, and match it to the blocks of time, encouraging you to break tasks into smaller elements (chunks) and finish them in the planned time periods.

Thoughts from my teacher 👨‍🏫

Paying attention to school-related tasks is cognitively demanding and can be neurologically exhausting. This is particularly true if you are trying to focus on something for long periods of time, or cram for hours on end. Like the body, the brain needs time to rest and recharge, and as such downtime during study sessions can prove invaluable. In fact, downtime resulting in boredom appears to assist students to function at their highest levels and is a necessary ingredient to develop creativity, awaken curiosity and perform optimally. In this sense, it is important to remember that although you may crave some sense of stimulation, it is important to find times to rest; a feeling of boredom is thus a good indicator to take some time to do nothing rather than looking for something to do. There is a growing body of scientific evidence suggesting that boredom is to the mind what sleep is to the body – a restorative state where new information can be synthesised and new neural connections wired (Bench & Lench, 2013). In other words, in order to get the most out of your attention and other cognitive resources when studying, you should plan for breaks and downtime and allow yourself to be bored more often.

A final word on thinking about attention spans

It is a smart strategy to accept that our brain does not focus well on one task for hours on end, and adapt our study to work with, rather than against, our attention spans.

References

Bench, S. W., & Lench, H. C. (2013). On the function of boredom. *Behavioral Sciences*, *3*(3), 459–472. https://doi.org/10.3390/bs3030459

Jensen, E. (2008). *Teaching with the brain in mind* (2nd ed.). Hawker Brownlow Education.

Memon, M. (2019, April 2). The science behind the pomodoro technique and how it helps supercharge your productivity. *focus booster blog*. https://www.focusboosterapp.com/blog/the-science-behind-the-pomodoro-technique/

CHAPTER 17

The role of sleep (and caffeine intake)

"

Sleep is an investment in the energy you need to be effective tomorrow.

Tom Rath, wellbeing consultant

"

The power of getting enough sleep

Perhaps the easiest way of thinking about the importance of sleep is to think about ourselves when we haven't had enough sleep: most of us are more inclined to be irritable, forgetful and less able to concentrate on what we need to do, none of which is good for learning. Getting enough sleep allows us to consolidate our learning, get ourselves ready to learn for the next day and even helps moderate levels of the stress hormone cortisol the following day.

How adequate sleep helps your learning (and the problem of too much caffeine)

For many people, part of the culture of study involves momentum that works against healthy sleep habits, with a mix of late nights, occasional all-nighters and the ever-present demands of competing priorities that might include part-time work at irregular hours or a social life, all while juggling a variety of other commitments. By itself, a pattern of irregular sleep is not good for learning. This is exacerbated if students start to rely on caffeine, whether in the form of coffee, cola, energy drinks or tablets, as caffeine use has the potential to further reduce sleep quality and negatively impact learning.

Jensen and Snider (2013) encourage students to cut down on caffeine to get adequate sleep. Sleep deprivation is a problem for many learners, and they warn that 'adequate sleep plays a critical role in memory consolidation' and 'sleep deprivation has a negative impact on the prefrontal cortex which regulates the executive function skills needed for academic success', two critical elements needed for effective learning (p. 121).

Clearly sleep is important. In fact, if you think about what you are trying to do as you cram your way through exams, a lack of sleep might be exactly what is standing in the way of learning. You cram hard to get the best possible results, but the lack of sleep means that you are not consolidating what you have learned and you will not learn as well the next day because you will be feeling more stressed and unable to concentrate. It seems to be a potentially frustrating loop that is best avoided.

Jensen and Snider (2013) recommend a variety of strategies to improve sleep, including removing electronics from your room, turning off the television 30 minutes before bedtime and computer, tablets and phones 60 minutes before sleep, reducing caffeine intake and keeping your bedroom cool and dark.

Building effective study skills and habits can be seen as analogous to creating a high-performance environment for learning. As high-performance athletes focus on sleep for recovery and ensure they are well rested before an event, sleep is an important part of supporting the high-performance learning environment.

The bottom line is that sleep is a powerful ally in the process of learning. It is important to keep this in mind as you think about your academic goals, the amount and quality of sleep you get and, in a world with more ways to consume caffeine in bigger quantities than ever before, your caffeine intake.

The evidence that convinces me of the importance of sleep to study

Harvard University and WGBH Educational Foundation (2007) have succinctly summarised the research on sleep:

> In the view of many researchers, evidence suggests that various sleep stages are involved in the consolidation of different types of memories and that being sleep deprived reduces one's ability to learn ... the overall evidence suggests that adequate sleep each day is very important for learning and memory. (p. 8)

This quote emphasises a particularly important element of sleep – the impact of sleep on your ability to concentrate and participate effectively in class. 'A sleep-deprived person cannot focus attention optimally and therefore cannot learn efficiently' (Harvard University & WGBH Educational Foundation, 2007, p. 7). A lack of sleep negatively affects your ability to both learn in class the next day and consolidate memories from the day before.

Thoughts from my teacher 👨🏻‍🏫

Science tells us something that most parents already know: teens stay up later than their younger siblings and, frequently, later than their parents. One of the reasons for this is a natural change in the timing and secretion of melatonin by the pineal gland during the teenage years. Melatonin is the neurotransmitter that induces sleep, and while there is plenty of scientific speculation as to why a teenage brain's melatonin fluctuates, there is little doubt of its impact: teenagers stay up later, find it harder to fall asleep and can find themselves in a chronic state of sleep deprivation.

Contemporary society may also be adding to sleep problems due to the rampant use of screen devices which emit bands of blue light that also impact the release of melatonin. The science also tells us that teenagers need, on average, a minimum of nine hours of sleep each night (Owens et al., 2010). Importantly, a recent study found that students who lost just one hour in their recommended sleep cycle had deficits in emotional functioning, short-term memory, working memory, attention and academic performance in comparison to those who had the required sleep (Vriend et al., 2013). In simpler terms, the sleepy students were often moodier and struggled with schoolwork.

There are, however, things that can be done to help regulate sleep in a positive fashion. The first is to limit the use of screen devices in the evening and keep technology out of the bedroom; the use of computers and smartphones should probably stop no later than 9 pm each night. Second, be sure to eat well and get plenty of exercise as both of these contribute to positive sleep patterns. And finally, if falling asleep is a problem, try reading (a book, not online), meditation or deep breathing when going to bed.

A final word on sleep and study

We could call it the 'sleep–study paradox'. During the busy times of the semester, we are trying our hardest to learn, but because of this we often don't get enough sleep – which impairs memory consolidation, impairs our ability to learn the next day and contributes to feeling more stressed. This is a great reason to ensure we are getting enough sleep to be in a position to learn well.

References

Harvard University & WGBH Educational Foundation. (2007, December 18). Sleep, learning, and memory. *Healthy Sleep*. http://www.elegantbrain.com/edu4/classes/readings/depository/TNS_560/sleep_procras/sleep.pdf

Jensen, E., & Snider, C. (2013). *Turnaround tools for the teenage brain: Helping underperforming students become lifelong learners*. Wiley.

Owens, J. A., Belon, K., & Moss, P. (2010). Impact of delaying school start time on adolescent sleep, mood and behavior. *Archives of Pediatrics and Adolescent Medicine*, *164*(7), 608–614. https://doi.org/10.1001/archpediatrics.2010.96

Vriend, J. L., Davidson, F. D., Corkum, P. V., Rusak, B., Chambers, C. T., & McLaughlin, E. N. (2013). Manipulating sleep duration alters emotional functioning and cognitive performance in children. *Journal of Pediatric Psychology*, *38*(10), 1058–1069. https://doi.org/10.1093/jpepsy/jst033

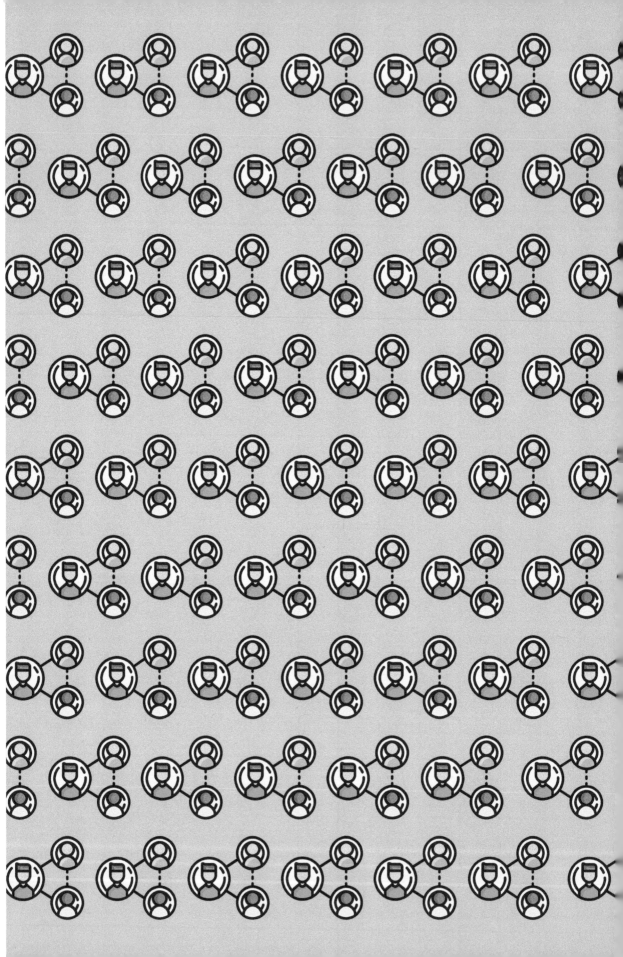

CHAPTER 18

The social brain
and studying with others

Alone we can do so little; together we can do so much.

Helen Keller, author and activist

The power of studying with others

We are often told that variety is important in life, and variety with our approaches to study may be able to help build our learning. One way of varying our study routine is by working with others. Studying with others gives us access to a variety of potential experiences that help our learning, as well as improving subject performance, understanding and confidence.

How to benefit from studying with others

Let's start by looking at some research around the core benefits that flow from learning with others, including allowing us to take different roles with our study and building positive results in terms of subject results, understanding, confidence and study skills. Hattie and Yates (2013) discussed how working with others extends the opportunity for learning by allowing different roles to be shared – asking questions, explaining content, ordering important information and finding links with other knowledge, which helps deepen understanding. There is also evidence, built from brain scans that measure brain function, that brain function increases in social settings, which in turn helps learning.

Michael Beasley (1997) argued that peer tutoring (effectively studying and learning with other students) results in improved:

- subject performance
- subject understanding
- confidence
- study skills.

That is an attractive list of benefits!

Learning with others also has other subtle benefits, including accountability (you show up for sessions because you do not want to let other people down) and the ability to learn from explaining the content and skills to each other. In terms of focus and attention, the extra stimulation of working with others means that you are less likely to zone out in a group setting.

So how might you use social learning for study that you are undertaking? It is a particularly useful tool for a subject that you are struggling with. Getting together with a study partner or small group of students who want to improve and meeting once or twice a week to revise would be a great strategy. In thinking about the practical application of the research on social learning, for example findings presented by Beasley (1997) that showed increases in results and confidence, it is worth noting that the benefits seem to come from meeting face-to-face, as opposed to virtually (for example, Skype or Zoom). This means that to benefit fully you need to make the effort to be working in a face-to-face environment, if circumstances allow.

In a school or university context, try to schedule the meetings for straight after class. That way, you will get the social benefit of learning *and* the benefit of tackling a challenging subject before you even get home.

However, there is a challenge in collaborative study that we should not gloss over. If meeting for an hour to work on a subject becomes a social hour, then the effort of meeting and working together will have no value. If you are not getting enough focused work done, this becomes a challenge for you to manage. Setting goals for what you want to accomplish in your time together, being honest about whether the time spent is valuable and being prepared to change something or walk away if it is not working for you are important parts of valuing your time as a student. That said, if you are working with people with common goals, then being prepared to nudge each other back on track should be something that is valued.

The evidence that convinces me of the value of studying with others

Lieberman (2012) considered the idea of the 'social brain' and how it can be used to enhance learning. He found that peer tutoring (studying and learning with your peers) may be the solution to engaging 'social motivations' (our desire to be with others) during the 'encoding of non-social information' (course content), commenting that 'multiple studies have demonstrated that peer tutoring benefits the educational attainment of both tutors and tutees' (Lieberman, 2012, p. 7).

Thoughts from my teacher 👨🏻‍🏫

Humans are social beings and, while schools are largely taken-for-granted aspects of society, the truth is that for much of human history education was a natural by-product of living and being with other people. So powerful is our innate need to be with others that solitary confinement is considered cruel and unusual punishment. Concomitantly, conceptions of the brain as a 'social organ' emerged only a few decades ago when neuroscientists began to discover that much of our physiology and biochemistry is deeply interwoven with our social relationships. Since that time, thousands of studies attest to the influence of social relationships on overall health and wellbeing, and learning (Cozolino, 2013). However, and in the context of this chapter, there are two important components linking social relationships, studying with others and learning. First, and as noted earlier, studying with others requires a level of discipline to stay on task and focus on getting the job done, whatever that job might be. And second, while social relationships are important, they must be founded on feeling safe, secure and trusted. Studying with others when tensions exist is counterproductive and, as such, it is important to ensure that all involved in studying together are happy to do so and that any issues are reconciled before working together.

A final word on studying with others

Provided you have the discipline to stay focused on the academic task at hand, learning with others is a great way to add some accountability, sociability and a variety of learnings skills into your study plan.

References

Beasley, C. J. (1997). Students as teachers: The benefits of peer tutoring. In R. Pospisil, & L. Willcoxson, (Eds.), *Learning through teaching: Proceedings of the 6th Annual Teaching Learning Forum, Murdoch University, February 1997* (pp. 21–30). Murdoch University. https://clt.curtin.edu.au/events/conferences/tlf/tlf1997/beasley.html

Cozolino, L. (2013). *The social neuroscience of education: Optimizing attachment and learning in the classrooms.* Norton Professional Books.

Hattie, J., & Yates, G. C. R. (2013). *Visible learning and the science of how we learn.* Taylor and Francis.

Lieberman, M. D. (2012). Education and the social brain. *Trends in Neuroscience and Education, 1*(1), 3–9. https://doi.org/10.1016/j.tine.2012.07.003

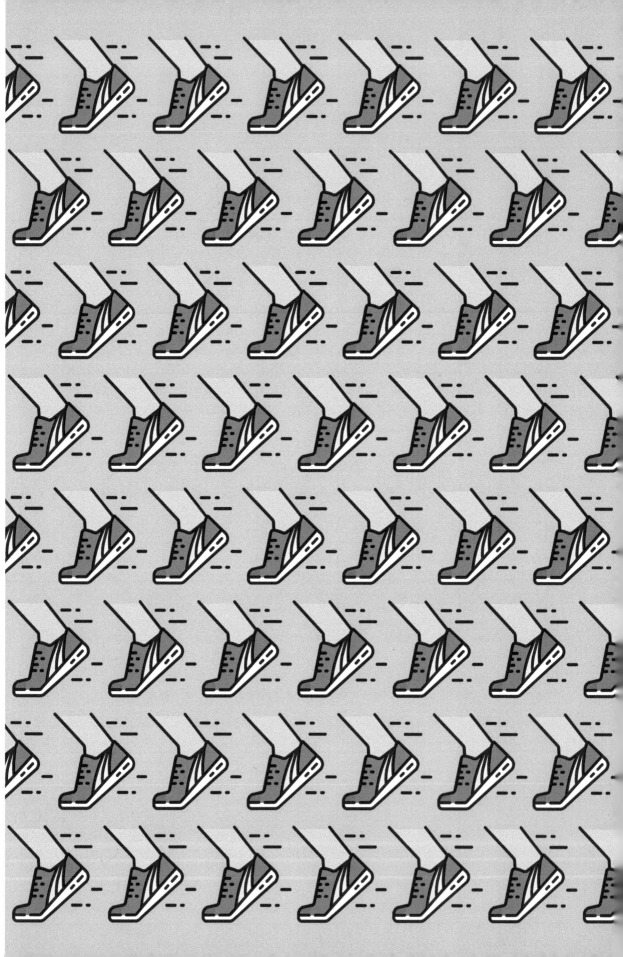

CHAPTER 19

The role of exercise

"

Never hurry. Take plenty of exercise. Always be cheerful. Take all the sleep you need. You may expect to be well.

James Freeman Clarke, theologian and author

"

The power of exercise as part of your study routine

Exercise has both short-term and long-term positive effects on brain function, including better mood and focus and improving brain structure. Both of these make exercise an important strategy to support your academic ambitions.

How to use exercise to enhance learning

Exercise is an important tool for helping with our learning. Let's start by having a look at some of the evidence about how exercise has positive short-term and long-term benefits for the brain.

Suomen Akatemia (2016) discussed the positive impact on learning that exercise is now accepted to have, including 'positive effects on brain structure and function, for example, the generation of neurons (neurogenesis) in the hippocampus, a brain structure important in learning' (para. 1).

Heidi Godman (2014) provides some more insight into this, saying that:

> The benefits of exercise come directly from its ability ... to stimulate the release of growth factors – chemicals in the brain that affect the health of brain cells, the growth of new blood vessels in the brain, and even the abundance and survival of new brain cells.
>
> Indirectly, exercise improves mood and sleep, and reduces stress and anxiety. ('Exercise and the brain' section)

Many studies of the relationship between exercise and learning have found positive links between aerobic exercise and learning. For example, one study by the University of British Columbia reported positive results for learning after participants walked for 60 minutes twice a week (Aldridge, 2015).

When we put this research together, we have a very positive picture of the impact of exercise on learning. However, many students tackling the challenges of Year 11 and 12 or university reduce the amount of exercise they do, for example dropping out of sporting teams. But why would you want to reduce an activity with these benefits at such an important time? Exercise, with immediate benefits that include improving mood and alertness and reducing stress, is the ultimate study break.

When you are struggling to concentrate on your work, unsure whether anything you are learning is actually 'going in', or just tired of study, then a brisk 10–20-minute walk would seem to be the ideal antidote. However, this is exactly the time that many students will instead reach for some caffeine, which might help with alertness in the short term, but then leads to troubles sleeping, as discussed in Chapter 17. A brisk walk instead of caffeine similarly improves alertness and mood in the short term, with long-term benefits that will also help you become a more effective learner.

The evidence that convinces me of the value of exercise

Let's go to a 'show me the money' example of research that considered the relationship between physical activity and academic results. Elmagd et al. (2015) found that there was a significant and positive relationship between physical activity and academic performance, with 20 per cent of the increase in the GPAs of students being explained by levels of physical fitness.

Thoughts from my teacher

Exercise creates fertilisers for the brain! For decades we have known about the overall benefits of exercise to our physical health, but we now know that exercise is an important consideration for brain health and functioning. It turns out that when you start exercising, your brain recognises this as a type of stress and, as your heart rate and blood pressure increases, the brain begins the fight-or-flight response. To protect the brain from stress, the body releases a type of protein, brain-derived neurotrophic factor or BDNF. BDNF activates brain stem cells to convert into new neurons and triggers numerous other chemicals that strengthen and protect neurons while promoting overall neural health. It also appears to strengthen neurons and is essential for synaptic plasticity, learning and those regions of the brain responsible for working memory (Nagel & Scholes, 2016). BDNF also provides 'a protective and also reparative element to your memory neurons and acts as a reset switch' (Widrich, 2012, 'What triggers happiness in our brain when we exercise?' section). That is why we often feel so at ease and like our thoughts are clearer after exercising and why BDNF is analogous to fertilisers for plants; it helps to build and maintain cell circuitry just as fertilisers strengthen the roots and structures of plants. Moreover, numerous studies have identified that physical activity, both acute or moderate, appears to enhance executive functioning in children and some studies indicate that when physical activity is coupled with executive functioning or 'thinking while doing', executive functioning is enhanced (Best 2010; Chaddock-Heyman et al., 2014; Davis et al., 2011; Guiney & Machado, 2013; Verburgh et al., 2014). In the end, it is apparent that physical activity positively affects cognition and as such can positively influence the very processes required for your learning and academic achievement.

A final word on exercise and study

When you are tackling study challenges, keep in mind that exercise supports your study endeavours while adding a little 'brain fertiliser' to the learning mix. Do not find yourself too busy to keep yourself fit and your brain working at its best!

References

Akatemia, A. (2016, February 8). Sustained aerobic exercise increases adult neurogenesis in brain. *ScienceDaily*. https://www.sciencedaily.com/releases/2016/02/160208083606.htm

Aldridge, F. (2015, July 23). Aerobic exercise is as good for the older brain as it is for the body. *The University of British Columbia*. https://news.ubc.ca/2015/07/23/aerobic-exercise-is-as-good-for-the-older-brain-as-it-is-for-the-body/

Best, J. R. (2010). Effects of physical activity on children's executive function: Contributions of experimental research on aerobic exercise. *Developmental Review, 30*(4), 331–351. https://doi.org/10.1016/j.dr.2010.08.001

Chaddock-Heyman, L., Hillman, C. H., Cohen, N. J., & Kramer, A. F. (2014). The importance of physical activity and aerobic fitness for cognitive control and memory in children. In C.H. Hillman (Ed.), *The relation of childhood physical activity to brain health, cognition, and scholastic achievement – Monographs of the Society for Research in Child Development* (pp. 25–50). Wiley-Blackwell.

Davis, C. L., Tomporowski, P. D., McDowell, J. E., Austin, B. P., Miller, P. H., Yanasak, N. E., Allison, J. D., & Naglieri, J. A. (2011). Exercise improves executive function and achievement and alters brain activation in overweight children: A randomized, controlled trial. *Health Psychology, 30*(1), 91–98. https://doi.org/10.1037/a0021766

Elmagd, M. A., Mossa, A., Sami, M. M., El-Marsafawy, T. .S., Al Jadaan, O., & Mudawi, M. S. E. (2015). The impact of physical activity on the academic performance among medical and health sciences students: A cross sectional study from RAKMHSU Ras Alkhaimah-UAE. *International Journal of Physical Education, Sports and Health. 2*(1), 92–95.

Godman, H. (2014, April 9). Regular exercise changes the brain to improve memory, thinking skills. *Harvard Health Blog*. https://www.health.harvard.edu/blog/regular-exercise-changes-brain-improve-memory-thinking-skills-201404097110

Guiney, H., & Machado, L. (2013). Benefits of regular aerobic exercise for executive functioning in healthy populations. *Psychonomic Bulletin & Review, 20*(1), 73–86. https://doi.org/10.3758/s13423-012-0345-4

Nagel, M. C., & Scholes, L. (2016). *Understanding development and learning: Implications for teaching*. Oxford University Press.

Verburgh, L., Königs, M., Scherder, E. J. A., & Oosterlaan, J. (2014). Physical exercise and executive functions in preadolescent children, adolescents and young adults: A meta-analysis. *British Journal of Sports Medicine, 48*(12), 973–979. https://doi.org/10.1136/bjsports-2012-091441

Widrich, L. (2012, August 28). What happens to our brains during exercise (and why it makes us happier). *lifehacker Australia*. https://www.lifehacker.com.au/2012/08/what-happens-to-our-brains-during-exercise-and-why-it-makes-us-happier/

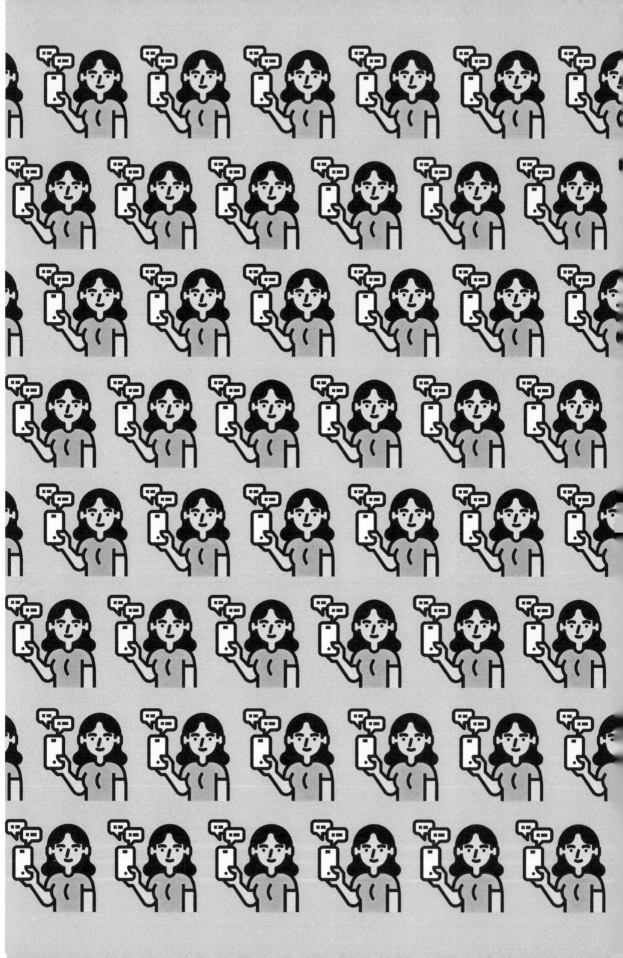

Multitasking: The challenge of study and Facebook and Instagram and YouTube and study and email and study and Twitter and study ...

Multitasking is merely the opportunity to screw up more than one thing at a time.

Steve Uzzell, *The one thing*

The power of avoiding multitasking

Having your attention divided amongst several activities at once reduces your effectiveness as a learner. If you can minimise distractions while you study, allowing yourself to focus on the task at hand, you have taken a significant step towards an effective study session.

How to avoid multitasking while studying

I suspect that you know where I am going to go with this chapter. Sitting down in front of a computer has more potential distractions than sitting at a notebook ever had. These distractions get in the way of learning in more ways than just the time that they take away from our study – the disruption impacts our trains of thought, and it takes us a surprising amount of time to get back to the task at hand.

The 'how' of this chapter is a challenge for everyone – we live in a time where we do not need to go any further than our phones for an array of distractions as diverse as watching cat videos to checking our bank accounts to seeing what our friends are up to. Deciding how you are going to manage distractions is a significant moment of truth in your study efforts.

At a practical level it is going to take a certain amount of discipline. That said, the pomodoro technique, which looks to use smaller, more intense periods of work time with frequent breaks mentioned in Chapter 16, might help you fit your distractions around your study. Rather than trying to grit your teeth and seemingly ignore the world for hours at a time, a quick break after 15 or 20 minutes means that you are never too far away from connectedness.

There is some significant research about how social media negatively impacts learning. For example, Rosen et al. (2013) looked at the actual study habits of high-school and university students, including monitoring the technologies that were present and web-browser windows that were open. The study observed on a minute-by-minute basis what students were doing. They found that, on average, students had less than 6 minutes (not 60, not 16, but 6 minutes) of on-task behaviour before becoming distracted (Rosen et al., 2013). The research also found that students who accessed social media during their study time had lower grade point averages (GPA).

Similarly, Gorlick (2009) reported that multitaskers had reduced ability to find key information, remember information and concentrate on processing tasks. All of these factors reduce a person's academic performance, and are largely the opposite of what we are trying to achieve while we study.

So, what can you do with this information? My suggestion is to clear your study time of social media and other distractions. When you are studying, study. Schedule breaks as you need them, even as frequently as every 15–20 minutes, to reconnect briefly with your distractions, but be 100 per cent committed to the task during your study blocks. We have talked a lot about the research around social media and study, as it is a source of distraction that can be observed and its impact calculated. Though it is not going to be the only distraction that is faced. This is where we need to be reflective as to the other distractions in our environment and manage those distractions. If home is chaotic and noisy, then the library after classes might be a better place to work. If the tendency is to watch television while trying to study, then finding an environment where this is not possible will remove this distraction. As learners, if we are serious about making the best use of our time then we need to be honest about the impact of all distractions that exist in our environment and be prepared to manage them.

The evidence that convinces me of the value of managing our multitasking

I became particularly aware of the perils of multitasking when attending a seminar on study skills. Those of us in the audience were asked to do a quick activity. We had to spell the word 'multitasking' and then count to 12, putting our hands up when we had finished. It took on average 3–4 seconds to do. Then we had to do it again, with a slight variation. We had to spell 'multitasking' again and, after each letter, number the letter from one to 12. So, this time it was 'm 1 u 2 l 3 t 4 i 5 …' It took more than twice as long – and showed that doing two simple tasks at once makes for one far more challenging task. This was a great, practical example of how multitasking reduces effectiveness.

Thoughts from my teacher 👨🏻‍🏫

The word *multitasking* is a bit misleading when it comes to the human brain. The brain is designed to pay conscious attention to one thing at time. So, while walking and chewing gum does not present any difficulties, walking while looking at your phone can be very dangerous, because you are failing to consciously attend to your surroundings. The truth of the matter is that the brain is only really capable of multitasking under two conditions. The first is that one or more of the tasks at hand must be second nature … there is not any real thought necessary to walk and chew gum. The second condition occurs when the tasks being performed involve different processes in the brain. For example, if you are reading or studying you can listen to instrumental music at the same time, but if the music has lyrics you are less likely to retain as much information. This is due to the fact that reading and listening to lyrics both engage language regions of the brain, making the retention of information difficult.

There is also growing evidence that multitasking, which is in essence trying to do too many things at once, can lead to increased anxiety, impact negatively on memory, inhibit creative thinking and cause more mistakes (Carrier et al., 2015; Courage et al., 2015; Glass & Kang, 2019; Rothbart & Posner, 2015). It should be self-evident that those are not great outcomes when it comes to any aspect of studying or scholastic endeavour. Finally, and as alluded to earlier in this chapter, multitasking, attention and distractions are closely linked and when you are trying to complete assignments, do homework or engage in most aspects of studying it is important to limit potential distractions so your brain can focus on the job at hand.

A final word on multitasking

The impact of distraction on learning is significant and negative. If we want to keep moving toward our academic goals while getting the biggest bang for our buck from our study time, then we have to be aware of the potential distractions in the environment, including social media, and make sure that they don't impact our learning.

References

Carrier, L. M., Rosen, L. D., Cheever, N. A., & Lim, A. F. (2015). Causes, effects, and practicalities of everyday multitasking. *Developmental Review*, *35*, 64–78. https://doi.org/10.1016/j.dr.2014.12.005

Courage, M. L., Bakhtiar, A., Fitzpatrick, C., Kenny, S., & Brandeau, K. (2015). Growing up multitasking: The costs and benefits for cognitive development. *Developmental Review*, *35*, 5–41. https://doi.org/10.1016/j.dr.2014.12.002

Glass, A. L., & Kang, M. (2019). Dividing attention in the classroom reduces exam performance. *Educational Psychology*, *39*(3), 395–408. https://doi.org/10.1080/01443410.2018.1489046

Gorlick, A. (2009, August 24). Media multitaskers pay mental price, Stanford study shows. *Stanford News*. https://news.stanford.edu/2009/08/24/multitask-research-study-082409/

Rosen, L. D., Carrier, L. M., & Cheever, N. A. (2013). Facebook and texting made me do it: Media-induced task-switching while studying. *Computers in Human Behavior*, *29*(3), 948–958. https://doi.org/10.1016/j.chb.2012.12.001

Rothbart, M. K., & Posner, M. I. (2015). The developing brain in a multitasking world. *Developmental Review*, *35*, 42–63. https://doi.org/10.1016/j.dr.2014.12.006

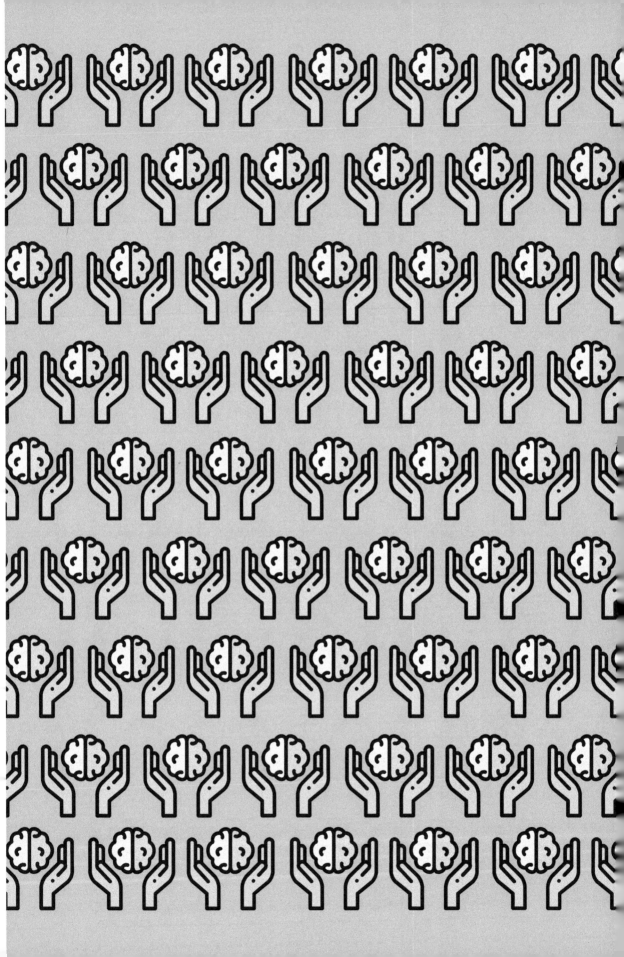

Milton Keynes UK
Ingram Content Group UK Ltd.
UKHW050642201123
432900UK00005B/48